DATE			
APR 2 9 1982			
FEB 7 1990			
MAY 2 3 1990			
FEB 1 4 1991			

© THE BAKER & TAYLOR CO.

The Land and People of
ZAMBIA

Zambia lies deep in the center of Africa and was one of the last parts of that continent to be opened to the outside world. The rich and complex culture of its people was drastically affected when Europeans began to arrive, imposing their own customs and exploiting the area's immense copper reserves. In the late nineteenth century, Great Britain took control of this territory, which became known as Northern Rhodesia.

In 1964, taking its new name from the mighty Zambezi River, Zambia courageously and nonviolently gained independence. Today, although experiencing many of the serious internal problems of emerging nations, Zambia is making great strides toward modernization under programs developed by her first president, Kenneth Kaunda.

Eliza T. Dresang introduces us to Zambia's unique wildlife and terrain, the fascinating history of the area from prehistoric times to the present, the traditional customs on which President Kaunda's philosophy of government is based, and the progress the nation has made since Independence.

PORTRAITS OF THE NATIONS SERIES

The Land and People of
ZAMBIA

by Eliza T. Dresang

PORTRAITS OF THE NATIONS SERIES

J. B. LIPPINCOTT COMPANY
Philadelphia   New York

ACKNOWLEDGMENTS

Grateful acknowledgment is made to the following: my husband, Dennis L. Dresang, for his encouragement and his expert advice as an African scholar; my friend, Linda West, for her invaluable critical comments; my parents, Dr. and Mrs. G. B. Timberlake, my parents-in-law, Mr. and Mrs. Norbert E. Dresang, and my children, Lee and Steve, for their support and understanding; the many Zambians without whom this book would have been impossible.

The author wishes to thank the following for permission to use the photographs in this book, on the pages listed below, and for their general willingness to help: National Archives of Rhodesia, pages 40, 54, 57, 59, 64; National Food and Nutrition Commission, pages 138, 140, 149; Nchanga Consolidated Mines, pages 112, 115, 117; Roan Consolidated Mines, page 109; Zambia Information Services, pages 11, 13, 15, 17, 21, 23, 32, 37, 46, 49, 69, 79, 83, 89, 94, 95, 101, 123, 124, 129, 132, 145, 146, 152, 155.

U.S. Library of Congress Cataloging in Publication Data

Dresang, Eliza T
  The land and people of Zambia.

  (Portraits of the nations series)
  Includes index.
  SUMMARY: Introduces the history, geography, people, and culture of the African country, once known as Northern Rhodesia.
  1. Zambia—Juvenile literature. [1. Zambia]   I. Title.
DT963.D73   916.89'4'034   74-23108
ISBN-0-397-31561-9

Map by Donald T. Pitcher

To my husband,
Dennis

Contents

1

African "Butterfly"

For many centuries man was puzzled and enticed by the mysteries locked in the heart of Africa. The territory which became the country of Zambia on October 24, 1964, was one of the last places to release its secrets to the curious outside world. Zambia lies virtually in the center of the part of Africa below the equator and is completely landlocked, so it was not easy to reach from north, south, east, or west. It took the religious zeal and burning curiosity of a great British explorer, David Livingstone, to open a path to this remote part of the continent.

During the twenty years following Livingstone's death in 1873, only a handful of Europeans, mostly missionaries, ventured into Africa's unknown center. Nonetheless, these years were crucial for the future of Zambia because of the "scramble for Africa" occurring in Europe. By the end of the nineteenth century, Britain had laid claim to the area of Central Africa from which Zambia would be carved. (Zambia was known as Northern Rhodesia prior to her independence from Great Britain.)

A quick glance at the map reveals that when the boundaries were firmly established in the early twentieth century, Zambia ended up with a most graceful and distinctive shape: the country resembles a giant butterfly posed in flight. It is symbolic of present-day Zambia's political ties that the butterfly seems to be flying away from the south and toward the north of Africa.

Zambia's long and irregular border is difficult to protect. Eight territories, some of which are openly hostile to Zambia, share her boundaries. Malawi is Zambia's neighbor to the east. To the north lie Tanzania (formerly Tanganyika) and Zaire (formerly the Congo); to the west, Angola; to the south, South-West Africa, Botswana and Rhodesia; and to the southeast, Mozambique.

Although Zambia's boundaries were determined politically, they make geographical sense. River systems and watersheds mark off the perimeters in long stretches.

Zambia derives her name from the mighty Zambezi River. It rises in the northwest and journeys to the south where it turns eastward and forms a five-hundred-mile-long border on its way to the Indian Ocean. This fourth largest river in Africa is notoriously shallow, filled with rapids, and completely unnavigable in some spots. Nonetheless, it has provided a vital trade route into Central Africa for many years. Both the Kafue River, winding its way down the center of the country, and the Luangwa, which isolates the Eastern Province from the rest of Zambia, are tributaries of the Zambezi.

Zaire is separated from Zambia by the long Zambezi-Congo watershed and by the Luapula River. The Luapula rises in Lake Bangweulu and cuts a path northward until it empties into Lake Mweru. The slow-flowing, listless Chobe River runs for 138 miles along the Angola-Zambia border, and the small Kalambo River, hardly more than a stream, forms a natural boundary between Zambia and Tanzania before it merges with Lake Tanganyika.

These boundaries enclose a land with an average altitude of between thirty-five and forty-five hundred feet. A wide, high plateau, sometimes called the backbone of Africa, slopes gently downward from its origins in South Africa to the lowlands of Central Africa three thousand miles to the north. The hot, steaming jungles usually associated with tropical Africa are not to be found in Zambia because of her position atop this plateau. The climate of Zambia is remarkably similar to that of southern California, but with more rainfall and less smog. The year is divided into three, rather than four, distinct seasons. The cool dry season, May to August, is followed by a hot dry season, September to November. Rain is almost unknown during these

The Zambezi River flows through typical flat savanna land above Victoria Falls.

months. Trees change colors and shed their leaves at the end of the cool months but almost immediately don their new greenery. From November to April, during the warm wet season, the dry, parched grass turns a vivid green. Average rainfall varies from fifty inches per year in the mountains of the northeast to twenty-five to thirty inches in the desert sands of the southwest.

Even in the cool season, the maximum temperature reaches to between sixty and eighty degrees Fahrenheit. During the hot season, highs range from eighty to ninety degrees Fahrenheit. Temperatures tend to be several degrees higher in the low-lying valleys.

In Zambia there are miles and miles of flat grassland sprinkled with trees, sometimes dense, sometimes widely spread. This typical African savanna and woodland cover approximately four-fifths of Zambia's land surface. All of Zambia's terrain is not so monotonous, however, for within the borders are to be found rugged mountains, majestic waterfalls, desolate sands, and soggy swampland.

Zambia is made up of eight provinces. Three of these—Luapula, Northern, and Eastern—lie in the eastern wing of the butterfly.

The vast and shallow Lake Bangweulu spreads over a portion of Luapula Province, home of the Lunda people. It is on the shores of this lake that David Livingstone died, still believing he had discovered the source of the Nile River. Although his body was returned to Westminster Abbey in England, his heart lies buried in this remote part of Zambia where he spent his last few years.

Bangweulu stretches on and on like an enormous mirror, and its name appropriately means "where the water meets the skies." In this part of Zambia are over three thousand square miles of water, mud, and swamps. The people who dwell here make their living from fishing. Near Samfya on the lake lies the only large rock in this swampland. In the past, villagers journeyed for as long as two days to reach this rock, on which they sharpened their knives and other tools.

Blindness strikes an unusually large number of the inhabitants of this province. Medical studies have connected the blindness to an infection spread by the monstrous crocodiles that reside in the swamplands.

Although the disease-bearing insects that flourish in Luapula Province make it an unhealthy environment for people, it is a marvelous place for wildlife and vegetation. Birds of all varieties abound. Purple orchids and pink lilies form living bouquets. In the swamps of Lake Bangweulu lives a species of antelope, the black lechwe, found nowhere else in the world. Scientists estimate that only fifty years ago there were over one million black lechwe in Zambia. Poachers have made their mark. Now there are only sixteen thousand black lechwe left.

Several large rifts, or splits, in the earth cut deep into the Zambian plateau. The steep walls of these valleys are known as escarpments. Lake Mweru lies in one of these valleys, fifteen hundred feet below the surrounding land. About one hundred miles to the east, far into the Northern Province, is an even deeper rift in which lies Lake Tanganyika, the longest and probably the deepest freshwater lake in the world. On the shores of Lake Tanganyika is Mpulungu, Zambia's only port. Mysteriously, the water level of Lake Tanganyika rose several feet in the early 1960s. It destroyed a recently built harbor works and fishing shed and forced villagers near the water to abandon their homes.

Hundred-pound Nile perch inhabit the waters of Lake Tanganyika, and fishing is a major local industry. The fishermen do not seem to bother the elephant and hippo which roam freely through the Sumbu Game Reserve on the shores of the lake.

A spectacular sight near the southern tip of Lake Tanganyika is Kalambo Falls. It is the highest sheer-drop waterfall in Africa

Kalambo Falls.

and the twelfth highest in the world. The Kalambo River looks like no more than a tiny ribbon of water as it plunges straight down 726 feet. The Kalambo gorge is a breeding ground for the ugly, vulturelike marabou stork, which is rarely seen elsewhere in Zambia.

To combat the poor soil of Northern Province, the Bemba people, the most numerous tribal group of the area, developed the *chitemene,* or the "slash and burn" method of agriculture. Branches are removed from trees and burned to enrich the ground. This method of fertilization, in combination with grass fires, which are common during the hot dry season, leaves large stretches of land charred and covered with ash. Trees are small and scrubby and the landscape is not one of great beauty.

The Eastern Province is separated from the Northern Province by the Muchinga Mountains, which include the highest points in Zambia. They are part of a great escarpment on the western edge of the Luangwa River valley and have peaks reaching up to eight thousand feet. The valley, in contrast, is low-lying, hot, and humid. The former lords of the land, the big game animals, still roam here in great abundance, unchallenged by human inhabitants. The only known white impalas in the world reside in the Luangwa Valley Game Park.

To the east of the Luangwa River, the terrain changes from flat savanna to rolling hills. Cashew nuts, tobacco, cotton, and maize (corn), cash crops, are grown in the fertile soil of the Eastern Province. Many of the first European farmers to arrive in Zambia settled here among the Ngoni people, creating one of the few densely populated rural areas of the country.

In the western wing of the Zambian "butterfly" are the remaining five provinces—Northwestern, Western, Southern, Central, and Copperbelt.

In the center of this wing, Kafue National Park sprawls over 8,650 square miles, half the size of Switzerland. It is one of the three largest game reserves in Africa. Buffalo in herds of more than one thousand, elephants, wildebeests (gnus), zebras, cheetahs, leopards, and spectacular birds fill the flat plains. The Zambian government is faced with the dilemma of attempting to preserve this area unspoiled—for nature here is still little disturbed by man—while encouraging tourism as a part of the general economic well-being of the country.

Throughout Zambia villages are sparsely populated and widely spaced, but Northwestern Province has the fewest people of all. The largest settlement, Mwinilunga, has fewer than four thousand people. The isolation of Northwestern Province from the rest of the country makes difficult the export of the juicy, golden pineapples that grow there. Few Zambians can benefit from this much-needed treasure. Patches of dry, low evergreen forest are another characteristic of Zambia's most remote province.

To the south, in the sandy Western Province, which borders on the Kalahari Desert of South-West Africa, the Lozi people live mainly along the banks of the Zambezi where they do a great deal of fishing. Annually in January the river floods the plains and forces the inhabitants to seek higher ground until the rains

A traditional fishing ceremony at Musukwe in Western Province.

end. The surface of the sands dries quickly, but underneath enough water is retained to support large forests of towering evergreen trees. The teak and mahogany forests of Western Province provide valuable timber for construction, flooring, furniture, and props in the mines.

The Zambezi flows onward into the Southern Province until it quite suddenly spills over a cliff and forms the most magnificent waterfall in the world. Great billowy clouds of mist rising in giant columns to the sky and the deafening roar of one million gallons of water per second crashing downward into a chasm inspired the Lozi people to give these falls the poetic name *Mosi-oa-tunya,* "the smoke that thunders." The name by which they are better known outside Zambia, Victoria Falls, was given to them by David Livingstone in 1855. While still six miles from the falls, he wrote in his journal that what he saw looked "exactly as when large tracts of grass are burned in Africa." On a clear day, the vapor is visible for more than twenty miles.

The Zambezi River is almost 6,000 feet across as it plunges downward for 347 feet, making Victoria Falls twice as wide and one and a half times as high as Niagara Falls in North America.

Rainbows paint the air above the falls, explaining another African name for them, *Chongwe,* "the place of the rainbow." Lush tropical growth lines paths on either side. The constant spray creates here the jungle usually associated with all of tropical Africa. Monkeys peer from the treetops and elephants wander not far away.

Below the falls, the mighty, swirling river crashes into the walls of a sheer cliff and must force its way into a narrow gorge. From the air, it appears that the falls are the top and the river beyond the bottom of a giant letter *T.*

Farther down the Zambezi, still in Southern Province, is Lake Kariba, the largest man-made lake in the world. It is 175 miles long, 20 miles wide, and covers an area of about 2,000 square miles. Kariba Dam, which backed up the waters of the Zambezi to form the lake, has more than the combined capacity of Shasta, Hoover, and Grand Coulee dams in the United States; it is 420 feet high and 80 feet thick.

Victoria Falls.

The construction of the dam in the late 1950s was both a blessing and a curse to the people of Zambia. The dam's main purpose was to supply much-needed power. In addition, irrigation of the land has made possible flourishing vegetable farms and fruit trees. Resort facilities and game reserves provide attractive vacation spots. However, the flooding of such a vast area of land meant the displacement of over forty thousand of the Tonga people and thirty thousand animals from their traditional homelands. Before the move was accomplished there was fighting between the police and the people in which eight Tonga were killed and thirty-four wounded. Over two thousand animals had to be carried from the islands in the middle of the lake where they were trapped. This feat, called "Operation Noah," received worldwide publicity.

Northward from Lake Kariba lies Central Province and the

site of the recently completed Kafue Dam. Lions roam in and above the narrow, steep-sided gorge where the river is harnessed. Farther upstream in the Central Province, the land around the Kafue River becomes very flat, and, indeed, is called the Kafue Flats. This grassland, covering over one million acres, was once, millions of years ago, the floor of a lake. Like the land around the Zambezi, it is flooded during the rainy season. Fewer trees grow here than anywhere else in Zambia.

A distinctive feature of both Southern and Central provinces is the herds of cattle, each including hundreds of cows. The commercial agriculture of Zambia is concentrated in these provinces. Large cotton cooperatives, for example, produce fibers for Zambian-made cloth.

Five hundred million years ago, a mountain range, the Katanga arc, ran through the Copperbelt Province, which lies to the north. Although the mountains were flattened during a subsequent ice age and are no longer visible, in their base is found the great mineral wealth of Zambia. The copper mines that dominate the landscape of this province have made Zambia the third biggest producer of copper in the world.

Dusty, red soil is characteristic of most parts of the country. However, fully 5 percent of the land is covered by patches of heavy, black soil called *dambos,* scattered throughout Zambia. These grass-filled depressions in the ground catch rainfall and remain wet all year. Livingstone first described the dambos as "sponges" in the earth. Although the soil is not as fertile as it looks, crops can be grown in these marshes even in the dry season, so they are important to the people.

Another remarkable feature of the Zambian countryside is the grotesque baobab trees, characteristic of lower and hotter regions of the country. Many legends surround these giants, whose trunks may have circumferences as large as sixty-five feet. One is that the baobab was the last tree God planted when he created the world and he was so tired that he mistook the roots for the branches and pushed it into the earth upside down. The gnarled branches make this legend seem credible. Some baobabs are as old as two thousand years. From their fruit comes cream of tar-

tar and fibers that can be woven into cloth. Oil is extracted from the seeds and used in cooking. Ropes and cloth are made from its bark and its wood is used for canoes. In the past, the great trunks have been hollowed out for homes.

The cities sprinkled throughout the Zambian landscape are much more important to the country than their number and size would indicate. Today an increasing number of Zambians are making their homes in the urban areas. How and why the cities have grown and developed stands out as an especially important aspect of twentieth-century Zambian history.

2

Cities—Promises and Problems

Today 40 percent of all Zambians live within twenty-five miles of a railway that enters the country at Victoria Falls in the south and runs northward to the Copperbelt Province. Along what Zambians call the "line-of-rail" lie the principal urban centers as well as the most heavily populated rural areas.

Again it is appropriate to think of Zambia in terms of a butterfly with the portion of the country bordering the railway as the body. The butterfly's head, at the northern end of the line-of-rail, contains what has become one of the richest copper-mining regions in the world and the most densely populated urban area of Zambia. For many years both the towns and the mines in the Copperbelt Province were dependent on the railroad, completed in 1909, for survival.

Seven of the eight largest cities or towns in the province grew up during the 1920s and 30s in connection with the opening and working of copper mines. Ndola, population 150,800, the capital of the province and third largest city in Zambia, is the exception. Long ago Ndola was a trading and slaving center. Now its chief role is as an administrative and distribution point, although an old mine within the city limits was reopened in 1970.

Most of the Copperbelt towns are in pairs. When a mine started operation, the mining authorities could not wait for the British officials to decide to provide needed services, so they created a town owned and run by the mine. As the colonial government did move in, another settlement, frequently with its own name, would grow up adjacent to the first and often would

Zambia's first railway crossed the Zambezi and entered Zambia on this bridge, built in 1905.

duplicate services. The dual, side-by-side township system has remained.

Kitwe, with a population of approximately two hundred thousand, is the largest city in the Copperbelt and the second largest in Zambia. What today is a modern city, and a healthy place to live, was started nearly half a century ago in the midst of a mosquito-infested swamp that covered most of the Copperbelt.

Prosperity and continued growth characterize the Copperbelt towns, but far to the southern end of the line-of-rail is a city struggling to stay alive. Livingstone, population forty-three thousand, was the original capital of Zambia and was long the site of a booming tourist trade from southern Africa. But the capital has been moved, political difficulties have made the tourist trade unreliable, and even the mighty Zambezi, as it roars toward Victoria Falls, has become foul with pollution. Although Livingstone is still a major distribution center for agricultural and timber products and some new industry has purposely located there, the prospects for vast development are dim.

Zambia's railroad, like all early rail lines, consists of a single track. There is a siding or extra loop of track every twenty miles where trains can pass each other as well as refuel with wood and water. Some four hundred miles north of Livingstone, near the Lenje village of Chief Lusaakas, such a siding was created in the first years of the twentieth century. So, almost by chance, a place was marked for Lusaka, the present capital (since 1931) and the largest city in Zambia. In 1908, the first building was raised. Lusaka today has a population of almost four hundred thousand, approximately the same as that of Fort Worth, Texas. The inhabitants claim it is the fastest-growing city in Africa.

Lusaka is a large, spread-out city with clean, clear air. It is a garden city, boasting streets lined with purple jacarandas, crimson flamboyant trees, bougainvillea and poinsetta bushes, guava and mango trees, and a rainbow bouquet of flowers. The sprawl of Lusaka, however, is a mixed blessing. In terms of open space and beauty, it is an advantage. For utilities and other public services, it presents a severe problem.

Although Lusaka is not in the exact geographical center of Zambia, it is the center of all major communication networks. Through the city runs the Great East Road on its way to Malawi and Mozambique. Cairo Road, a broad thoroughfare along which the business district is located, is part of the Great North Road to Tanzania, Kenya, and Zaire.

On either side of Cairo Road are supermarkets, banks, chemists (drugstores), and bookshops. In contrast to the city sidewalks is a broad tree-lined strip running the length of Cairo Road directly down the center; on this peaceful oasis under the pod mahogany trees sit the curio sellers, endlessly polishing their carvings and other artifacts from Zambia, Zaire, and East Africa. With business going briskly on its way to either side, the traders are content to bargain with a prospective customer for as long as his patience holds out.

Widely spread throughout the rest of the city are the buildings that house the various ministries and other government offices. Sitting atop the hill where Chief Lusaakas lived and a dazzling sight in the bright sunshine of tropical Africa is the National Assembly Building with its gleaming copper dome. The copper was a gift from the mining companies at the time of Independence. Stones from every district in Zambia, except one, are a part of the building, a symbol of national unity. Kalambo, the one exception, had to send wood as there are no rocks in that district.

No African city would be complete without its marketplace. Near the center of Lusaka is the main market, a rather dull place both because of the lack of fresh produce—difficult to obtain anywhere in Zambia—and because of the absence of socializing. In the past this was known as the European market; the atmo-

Cairo Road, the main thoroughfare of Lusaka.

sphere is more formal than that of the markets farther out where Africans gather to trade and talk. There, the air is filled with bargaining, the squawking of chickens, and the odor of *kapenta,* a small dried fish that is a staple of the Zambian diet. Seamstresses, barbers, and bicycle repairmen rely on the market traffic for their livelihood.

Lusaka is a quiet city compared with the hustle and bustle and constant noise of many cities in western or northern Africa. Work starts early in the morning and, with a break of an hour and a half for lunch, continues until four in the afternoon. At night, except for the movement of cinemagoers, the muffled beat of tribal drums, and the monotonous moan of radios, the city falls silent. Nightclubs and flashing neon lights have yet to penetrate this part of Africa. Except in the large hotels and in a few smaller bars, there is little organized entertainment after dark.

But what of the people who inhabit these cities? Who are they and how do they live?

The population of Zambia in 1974 was estimated to be 4.5 million. (The last official census was in 1969.) Zambia is larger than the state of Texas but has only one-third as many inhabitants. The people are spread out over 290,586 square miles of territory, averaging only 15 per square mile. Approximately 64,175 or 1.42 percent of Zambia's inhabitants are not Africans, a high percentage in comparison to the less than 1 percent non-Africans in Ghana or Nigeria but not so high as that of Kenya where almost 3 percent of the population is non-African.

The 43,390 Europeans* represent thirty countries of origin, but most are English-speaking people from either Great Britain or South Africa. At present there is much coming and going as experts in various fields arrive in Zambia to work two to four years on a specific project, such as a road or railroad, or in an occupation for which not enough Zambians have been trained.

---

* "European" is a term used throughout Africa to mean any white person, be he from Europe, South Africa, or North America, etc. It is in this sense that the term will be used in the rest of the book. Likewise, "African" is used here to mean an African with black skin.

When the task is completed, these outsiders return to their homes but are usually replaced by other specialists for whom Zambia has a need. The other 10,785 non-Africans are Asians. The non-African population is especially pertinent to a discussion of Zambia's cities because most non-Africans live in urban areas, especially those on the Copperbelt.

Unlike the Asians and Europeans, the majority of Zambians do not live in cities. However, throughout the world, cities lure young people in large numbers from the rural areas with the enticements of better employment, more conveniences, and more opportunities of almost every kind. The cities of Zambia are no exception. Copper mining, particularly, has always seemed glamorous to many young people and the money, indeed, is there. Despite the fact that only 30 percent of the Zambian population had reached the cities by the early 1970s (contrasted with 73 percent in the United States), the trend is decidedly away from rural and toward urban living.

The promises of the cities are real, but so are the problems. Lack of adequate housing, schools, and jobs faces many newcomers, making it even more difficult for them to cope with a new way of life and rapid social change. Many find their pot of gold, but quite a few do not.

One of the most difficult problems for the African newcomer to the city is how to adjust to a nontribal way of life. The whole issue of tribalism is basic to any understanding of Africa, traditional or modern, and is worthy of a pause here to make its meaning clear.

Historically, tribes in Africa were kinship groups sharing common language, customs, and territory. Within the larger tribal groups were smaller family units known as clans. The customs of a person's tribe affected all that he did in life and his loyalty was to his tribe above all else. Tribe, incidentally, is considered a demeaning or derogatory term by some non-Africans who regard it as a word describing a part of Africa's past that present-day Africans prefer to forget. The Africans, themselves, use the term freely and without negative connotations.

Now that Africa is comprised of nations, the emphasis is on

loyalty to one's country above one's tribe. In many countries this break with past tradition has not been accepted by the people. Fierce rivalry among various tribes is often found, and frequently there is discrimination of one tribe against members of another in the same manner that racial discrimination is practiced in some places.

Although the migration of many young people to the cities has weakened tribal rituals, it has often intensified tribal loyalty. In a strange place, without friends or family, a new arrival turns to the only people with whom he can identify, members of his tribe. (Frequently people from a certain geographical area consider themselves members of the same tribe, even though historically this was not true.)

The banding together of members of a tribal group, both within the cities and without, is a problem with which Zambia has constantly grappled since Independence. It is not easy to find a solution that will carry on the positive aspects of tribal life and leave behind those which are not good for the country as a whole.

An extremely important aspect of African tribal life was sharing individual resources with the entire community. An example of the problems this philosophy can cause when only one family member has moved to a city can be found in what was perhaps the first advice column in Africa. The "Dear Abby" of Zambia was known as "Josephine," and letters written to her column, begun in 1960 in the *Central African Mail* (now the *Zambian Mail*), have been compiled, along with commentary by Barbara Hall, into a book called *Tell Me, Josephine.* "Dear Josephine," wrote one young man,

> I am well-known, and with a big family to feed. My house is by the bus-stop and every day I receive visitors from the home village. It is my duty to give my tribes-folk food and money for their journey needs. But my family suffers from hunger and I go without the decent clothes my position calls for. Though I have a good job I am kept poor by home-people. I do not

dislike them, but what can I do to be safe from them?

Inadequate housing is another intense problem in the cities of Zambia. Around the outskirts of the major cities have grown up areas known as compounds. Usually these are not recognized as legal settlements by the government, so no water, electricity, sanitary facilities, or health services of any kind are provided.

In the Kalingalinga compound, a typical one near Lusaka, the greatest need is for water. In the sweltering heat, a woman spends hours each day walking two or three miles to and from a rock quarry, the nearest source of water, balancing a large water jar on her head, usually carrying a baby tied to her back, and with a toddler or two by her side.

Shaggy dwellings are either the pole and *dagga* (mud) type with thatched roofs found in the villages or are made of metal sheets thrown together. There are no windows. Cooking is done over an open fire. Families are crowded together two or three to a one- or two-room house. The houses are close together and built in a haphazard fashion. Any road scheme is next to impossible.

Frequently a person who has been fortunate enough to get a job in the city and earns enough money to move elsewhere becomes an absentee landlord. Unfortunately, memories of past conditions fade rapidly. Little is done to improve the lot of the newly arrived.

Within the city limits houses range from the simple to the luxurious. Concrete blocks and Kimberley bricks (large blocks made from clay) are the most commonly used building materials. The round mud hut of the village gives way to the square or rectangular house of the urban area. Out of 87,900 houses in Zambia, only 24,000 are privately owned, so renting is widespread.

The cities along the line-of-rail in Zambia are products of the twentieth century. Often it is difficult to think of Africa in terms of skyscrapers and stock markets, but these are a very real part of Africa today. Perhaps easier to accept is the image of Africa in terms of the more familiar village life of centuries past.

3

Setting the Stage for History

Benjamin Franklin suggested, and others have accepted, that "man" is a creature who can both *make* and use tools. Scientific evidence strongly supports the theory that the first men in the world, according to this definition, evolved in Africa. Fossils of *Homo habilis* or "handy man," who lived over 1.8 million years ago, have been found in Tanzania. (The only older human fossil was uncovered in Kenya in late 1972 by Richard Leakey and Dr. Glynn Isaac. Its estimated age is 2.5 million years.) Although no skeletons of *Homo habilis* have been unearthed in Zambia, pebble tools of the type he used have been discovered near Lusaka. This finding suggests that from the dawn of man's existence, he has lived in what is now Zambia.*

The Stone Age—divided into early, middle, and late periods—began and ended at different dates in different parts of the world, according to the activities of the men in a certain region at a given time. The Stone Age in Zambia began approximately 1.8 million years ago and lasted up to the arrival of Iron Age farmers from the north between 150 B.C. and A.D. 1500.

Archaeological sites at both Kalambo Falls and Victoria Falls

* The area that is now Zambia was not a cohesive political unit until it became Northern Rhodesia in the early twentieth century. Moreover, there was no term that was used specifically to refer to the region. "Central Africa" designated a much broader part of the continent. Therefore, throughout this book, although it is not completely accurate to do so, the term "Zambia" will be used to refer to the geographical area that is present-day Zambia, except when discussing the historical period during which it was known as Northern Rhodesia.

contain the most information about the Zambian hunters and fishermen of the early Stone Age. The very earliest men did not live in caves, as people sometimes think, because they did not have weapons with which they could drive out the fierce animals who resided there. Their homes were in the open, always near water.

Between 50,000 B.C. and 40,000 B.C. men learned how to use fire, developed a wide range of tools, and moved into caves. The skull and skeleton of a middle Stone Age Zambian caveman was discovered by a terrified workman in 1921 during blasting at the Kabwe (formerly Broken Hill) lead and zinc mine. This find caused great excitement throughout the world. The remains of "Broken Hill man" or *Homo rhodesiensis,* as he came to be called, are the earliest that have ever been found in south central Africa. He is believed to be closely related to the famed Neanderthal man of Europe, western Asia, and North Africa. The body of Broken Hill man was quite similar to our own, but his mouth was larger, his neck was shorter and thicker, and he had almost no forehead. With a height of close to six feet, he towered over other Stone Age people. Broken Hill man may have been the first in Zambia to communicate by means of language. Spread over the vastness of the land of Zambia at this time was a population of approximately five thousand. (A study of types and dates of tools and other objects found at archaeological sites throughout Zambia allows scientists to estimate the number of people who lived there at any given time.)

While the Pharaohs were reigning in faraway Egypt and the pyramids were under construction, Zambia was inhabited by Bushman hunters of the late Stone Age. We know quite a lot about these people because some of their descendants are living today in much the same way as their ancestors did. The shy Twa people, part Bushman, part Pygmy, who inhabit the swamps of north and central Zambia, and the mysterious nomads of the extreme southwest near the Kalahari Desert have changed their way of life little in the past six thousand years.

Cave paintings are another source of information about the Bushmen of the past. Most of the rock art in Zambia is found in the eastern half of the country. Paint was made from natural materials: charcoal, red clay, and birdlime mixed with animal fat or egg. Berries provided dye.

The Bushman artists painted two kinds of pictures. Their naturalistic paintings represent scenes from everyday life. Often animals as well as people and objects appear in the black or purple drawings. Their schematic paintings, however, are much more numerous and are a more sophisticated type of rock art. Dots, circles, lines, and rectangles are splashed onto the cave walls in yellow, red, white, and brown. Some archaeologists interpret the signs and symbols as a form of magic in which the Bushmen believed. Perhaps they hoped to protect themselves against evil spirits or to bring luck in hunting or fighting.

During the late Stone Age, starting around 7500 B.C., wild animals no longer freely preyed upon man. The Bushmen had perfected the use of poisoned darts and had become accomplished marksmen with bows and arrows. These skills were used both in defense and in hunting for food. However, the Bushmen had no knowledge of either farming or the domestication of animals.

Approximately two thousand years ago, about the time of Jesus Christ, the first important wave of Bantu immigrants swept into Zambia from the north. Most Zambians of today are Bantu people, so it is important to understand what the term means. "Bantu" does not refer to a racial group or to a tribe. Rather, it describes a large group of African peoples whose languages are similar. Specifically, the term "Bantu" is applied to all peoples who use the word *ntu* to mean human being. *Ba* is simply a prefix that makes a word plural, as *s* does when added to the end of an English word. Therefore, *bantu* means human beings, or people.

Bantu-speakers are spread over most of eastern and central Africa. The Bantu languages are structurally and historically related, yet are distinct. In Europe there are similar linguistic groupings, such as the Romance languages. The four hundred Bantu dialects differ from one another as do Italian, French, and Spanish.

The original Bantu immigrants were early Iron Age people who no longer relied merely upon implements of stone but knew how to smelt and use iron. The Zambian Stone Age gradually ended with their arrival. The iron workers were also Zambia's first farmers and cattlemen, and the knowledge they brought caused a radical and lasting change in prehistoric Zambian life.

During the Iron Age, people no longer had to roam from place to place in a desperate search for food as had earlier inhabitants of Zambia. They formed villages around fertile farmlands and moved only every five to ten years when the soil ceased to produce. For the first time, people began to live in small, round huts instead of in caves or simple shelters. The huts, with their cone-shaped thatched roofs, were much like those found in rural Zambia today. Often the huts were arranged around an enclosure or kraal in which the domestic animals—cattle, sheep, and goats—were kept. During their leisure time the people made pottery and developed other arts and crafts.

The greatest concentration of early Iron Age peoples was in the present-day Southern Province. The Kalomo people, now extinct, once covered much of this area and are one of the most famous Iron Age communities that existed in southern Africa.

In 1960, workmen who were putting up a storage tank for water some thirty miles down the Zambezi from Kariba Dam uncovered what turned out to be an extraordinary settlement dating back to A.D. 650. On this site, called Ingombe Ilede, "place where the cow sleeps," archaeologists have found seashells, gold and glass beads, cloth and copper bracelets, all belonging to a wealthy and prestigious people. Some of these items were brought to the central Zambezi valley from great distances, some from as far away as India. Ingombe Ilede was in the center of one of the earliest trade routes into Central Africa. Arab traders sought ivory from the numerous elephants in the area, slaves to take to the coast, and copper that the Ingombe Ilede people obtained from tribes to their north. Small seashells (mpande shells) were used for currency. Two shells would purchase a slave and

A skeleton found at Ingombe Ilede, wearing copper bracelets and earrings.

five an elephant tusk. Pottery made by these people was as delicate and fine as modern bone china.

The Ingombe Ilede civilization peaked around A.D. 900. The settlement, apparently, broke apart sometime during this century, possibly when the merchants moved farther south to the more lucrative gold trading routes.

Three hundred years later, around A.D. 1200, another group of Iron Age Bantu people, the Tonga, Ila, and Lenje, settled close to the Ingombe Ilede site. On the farmland of this plateau area of southern Zambia, these three tribes—sometimes called the *Bantu Botatwe* (three people) because of their similarities—grew cereal crops and perhaps cotton, as had their predecessors, the farmers of Ingombe Ilede.

Unlike other tribes, the Tonga never formed a unified group ruled over by a single chief. Villages were extremely small and even slave raids against them in the nineteenth century did not cause the people to unite.

In the past, the Tonga and their neighbors distinguished themselves physically by knocking out their six upper front teeth, by piercing their noses with ivory sticks or bones, and by distending their lower lips with large, round discs. The latter custom was practiced only by the women. Some say these rituals were performed to frighten those who wanted to take them as slaves.

Perhaps the most important figure in the Tonga culture was the rainmaker. The Bantu peoples brought cattle into Zambia when they migrated and the Tonga were (and are) one of the major cattle-keeping peoples of Zambia, as well as being farmers, so rain for pastures and crops was of paramount importance. When a man announced that the spirits had appointed him to be a rainmaker, the villagers built or chose a shrine for him. Here he led the people in a spectacular annual ritual that involved endless hours of prayers and strenuous dances to please the spirits. Sometimes the ritual was repeated if the rains failed to come.

Marriage was very important to the Tonga man. Without a wife to brew beer for him, it was thought that he could not approach his ancestral spirits. If a man had more than one wife, he built adjacent huts for them. At mealtime the men and boys gathered to eat around one pot and the women and girls around another.

The Tonga, at least in some areas, have resisted change more intensely than other tribal groups. Some of their traditions have been held intact longer. Fewer Tonga have moved to cities; some have been reluctant to accept new methods of health care. On the other hand, the Tonga have entered the cash economy, selling their cattle and crops more readily than their neighbors the Lozi. It was the Tonga people who had to be moved during the creation of Lake Kariba. This dislocation disrupted a centuries-old way of life for many of them.

Although the origins of the Tonga are uncertain, it is thought that they entered Zambia from the north in the area around Lake Tanganyika. Between A.D. 1200 and A.D. 1600 other small tribal groups moved into what is now Zambia. However, the vast migrations that brought the ancestors of most present-day Zambians into the territory took place in the past three hundred years. The stronger tribes conquered the weaker peoples in the areas where they settled. The captives were sometimes assimilated but not always. Each of these migrating tribes had its own culture. Many of them have dropped their traditional practices little by little over the past eighty or ninety years until today's rural Zambian village is a mixture of African and European architecture, facilities, farming methods, and customs.

The knowledge we have of the Tonga comes from the first-hand observations of laymen and from studies done by anthropologists. For other Zambian tribes there is also another significant source of information known as oral history. Traditions and legends have been passed down for generations by word of mouth. A specific individual in a tribe was designated as the historian and often he could trace a tribe's history back to the beginnings of time. In the past few decades, many of these histories have been written down and from them has been gleaned valuable data. No one is certain why the Tonga have few oral traditions; perhaps it is because they have lived in small, isolated groups and have no lineage of chiefs to perpetuate.

Oral history is not completely accurate, of course, but it always contains some elements of truth. Much of what we know about the early history of Zambia is based on accounts that Zambian peoples have given of their past.

4

Kingdoms of the Past

At the time when the Industrial Revolution was spreading through Europe and the covered wagons were rolling westward over the plains in the United States, four great kingdoms were flourishing in Zambia. The Lozi of the Western Province, the Bemba of the Northern Province, the Lunda of the Luapula Province, and the Ngoni of the Eastern Province had carved out their separate spheres of influence. All were Bantu peoples.

The Africa of the past was much more sophisticated than is generally realized. Government was orderly and highly developed. Fighting was not haphazard, but carefully planned and skillfully carried out. Civilization flourished even before the Europeans "introduced" it.

Each of the four empires was ruled by a paramount chief who had many lesser chiefs or headmen under him. He reigned not only over his own tribe but over many smaller tribes as well. Most of the seventy other tribes of Zambia were at some time conquered by one of these four major powers. Three of the four tribes have legends that trace their origins to the vast empire ruled by the Lunda and Luba tribes of the Congo, who are thought to be descended from west African tribes.

The Lozi were the first of the four to enter Zambia, early in the seventeenth century, at approximately the same time that a small band of colonists from Great Britain set foot on American soil at Jamestown. As the Lozi tell it, a handsome chief of the Luba, who was a great and mighty hunter, tracked an animal one day deep into the territory of the Lunda. Here he encountered a beautiful chieftainess of the Lunda, and they immediately fell in love. The resulting marriage, which merged the Lunda and Luba peoples into one, displeased many of the Lunda men, who resented the idea of being ruled by a foreigner. In a rage these men took their families and moved to the east and the south and settled in what is now Zambia. The descendants of one of these families are the Lozi. (There is currently a debate among African historians as to whether the Lozi came from the Congo or penetrated Zambia from the south. If the latter is true, it would be one of the rare instances when oral traditions, which say they came from the north, have little to do with the actual origins of a people.)

The ruler of the Lozi is known as the *Litunga,* "keeper of the earth." The Litunga had, and still has, the most elaborate court in Zambia. Each year, usually in January, when the rains have caused the swelling of the Zambezi and the flooding of the plains, the Litunga moves from his dry season capital of Lealui to his wet season capital on the mainland, Limulunga.

This ceremony, called the *Ku-omboka,* unfolds with much pomp and circumstance. The Litunga heads the procession across the floodwaters, seated in the royal barge under a billowy white canopy. The forty paddlers of the barge are all princes and councillors wearing headdresses with flowing feathers. Following the Litunga is a second barge carrying the national drums. These royal drums, some of which are four hundred years old and as tall as a man, must be played throughout the journey. When the people hear the drums, they know all is well with their leader. The commoners complete the procession in dugout canoes, with the cattle swimming beside them.

So important was the Litunga to the Lozi that when he died, his favorite *indunas* (chiefs) had their arms tied behind their backs and plunged into the water, drowning themselves to express their great sorrow. All fires were extinguished until a new Litunga was chosen. The drowning no longer occurs, but the Litunga is still revered by many of his people.

Several Litungas achieved lasting fame as individuals. Mulambwa, who ruled from 1780 to 1830, is remembered for the

The royal barge carries the Litunga and his retinue to Limulunga.

unusual code of laws he formulated. One law stated that a person would steal only when he was in need. Thus, instead of punishing a man caught thieving, the king should present him with a cow or perhaps some land.

Another interesting Litunga, Lewanika I, 1842–1916, is the subject of a book-length biography by Gervas Clay. During the early part of his reign, the Lozi were conquered by the Makololo people from Rhodesia. A man who had once been David Livingstone's cook was responsible for overthrowing the Makololo and restoring Lewanika I to power in 1864. In his remaining years as Litunga, he consolidated a vast empire, ruling at one time over twenty-five different tribes.

Lewanika I was a ruler of great character. He was one of the only paramount chiefs who opposed the slave trade. Under him the vanquished tribes were treated as equal by the Lozi and there was a law which stated that no one was to be referred to as a foreigner.

The Lozi were one of the few African peoples whose villages remained in the same locations year after year. When they first reached Zambia, the Lozi built their dwellings on mounds that rise from the plains, and there they have remained. By living on the highest ground possible, they could shorten the period of time the floodwaters would force them to be away from their homes.

The Bemba people also broke off from the Lunda-Luba empire, but they did not arrive in Zambia until almost a hundred years after the Lozi, around the beginning of the eighteenth century. They have a legend about their origins that is, in some ways, similar to the biblical story of the Tower of Babel.

The two sons of a certain Luba chief directed the people to build a tower that would reach the sky. Each day it grew higher, but, unknown to the workers, termites were eating the wooden supports at the bottom. Unexpectedly, the tower collapsed with an earthshaking crash, and all the people were killed. The anger of the chief was so fierce that the two sons fled across the Luapula River and into what is now Zambia's Northern Province. One of the sons, Chiti, became the first paramount chief of the Bemba, and, ever since, their chief has had the title *Chitimukulu*.

The lineage of the Chitimukulu can be traced back twenty-six generations. Like the Litunga of the Lozi, he is much revered by the people. When he approaches, they kneel and throw dust upon themselves to show respect. After his death, the Chitimukulu's body is mummified and lies in state for an entire year before burial.

The Bemba tribe is divided into thirty clans. Each clan has the name of an animal, a vegetable, or a natural phenomenon, such as rain. The Chitimukulu and all the lesser chiefs belong to the crocodile clan, and so are called the "crocodile kings." All members of this clan have royal blood.

In the past, the men of the Bemba saw themselves as mighty hunters and warriors and bragged that they could not use a hoe. They were a tall, strong people who took much pride in their traditions. The small amount of farming that occurred was left to the women. Unlike most other Central African tribes, the Bemba kept no cattle.

Until the late nineteenth century, the chiefs lived mainly on the tributes paid to them by their subjects and on goods received from the Arabs in return for slaves. The Bemba and the Lunda were the two Zambian peoples most involved in the slave trade.

The Lunda crossed into Zambia from the Congo at approximately the same time that the Bemba did. Their paramount chief was known as the *Kazembe*. The capital of the Lunda in the Luapula Province with a population of twenty thousand was the largest settlement in Central Africa and lay in the middle of major trade routes running both east and west. It was a center for the trading of cloth, ivory, slaves, copper, firearms, and salt.

An early nineteenth-century Portuguese explorer described the reigning Kazembe as a cruel, but extremely colorful ruler. He wore a headdress in the shape of a pyramid, over a foot and a half high and made of brilliant feathers. Seven umbrellas, placed on tall bamboo poles and wrapped with cloths of many hues, shaded him from the sun.

The Lunda considered themselves superior to all other tribes. There was no attempt at equality such as was found among the Lozi. The other peoples of their domain were rarely allowed to participate in the Lunda rituals or, in any sense, to become a part of the Lunda culture.

The fourth large tribal group, the Ngoni, invaded Zambia from the south in the nineteenth century. Far away from Zambia in the southernmost part of Africa, Shaka, a powerful Zulu chief, was attempting to bring that entire portion of the continent under his ironclad rule. His *impis,* or warriors, showed no mercy to the peoples they ruthlessly attacked. Following their leader, Zwangendaba, a band of Zulu known as the Ngoni fled northward to escape the tyranny of Shaka's rule.

As the old men of the villages tell it, the Ngoni had displeased their ancestral spirits, so that as they crossed the Zambezi, the spirits extinguished the sun and sent a mighty flood as punishment. The Ngoni were panic-stricken; many of them and all of their cattle were drowned. Educated estimates can be made about the dates when most of the tribes entered Zambia, but the story of the darkened sun makes the Ngoni the only tribe for which an exact date is known. History records a total eclipse of the sun on November 20, 1835. Thus, a combination of fact and legend enables us to pinpoint the arrival of this tribe.

The Ngoni had what was, perhaps, the most highly organized of all the kingdoms. All men were a part of the complex and efficient military organization. The Ngoni brought with them the Zulu battle techniques. The warriors formed a long arc-shaped

A Ngoni warrior.

line. As a unit they rushed upon their enemy, attacking with short spears rather than with bows and arrows. They were the terror of the more settled people around them.

Since both the Ngoni and the Bemba were formidable fighters, it was inevitable that they should come into conflict as the Ngoni moved north. Ultimately the Bemba pushed the Ngoni back into the present-day Eastern Province, where they have stayed. The decisive factor in the battles was the gunpowder supplied to the Bemba by the Arabs in exchange for slaves. (The stronger African tribes sold as slaves their captives from weaker tribes.) The spears of the Ngoni were no match for the firearms of the Bemba. The Ngoni, however, maintained their military strength, and the Bemba did not attempt further southward expansion.

The Ngoni kept cattle, farmed, and hunted when they were not involved in battle. Attendance at a royal hunt was compulsory for all able-bodied men who were invited. Groups of villagers from different locations often joined together for dancing and beer drinking. The Ngoni mixed freely with the peoples they ruled.

The other tribes of Zambia also migrated from areas outside the country. Quarrels within the tribes, similar to the ones depicted in the Lozi and Bemba legends, were a major reason for the migration of peoples into Zambia. Others retreated from the devastating attacks of slave raiders.

During the seventeenth and eighteenth centuries, the sweet potato, maize (corn), cassava, and other new crops were being introduced to Africa by the Portuguese, who brought them from their colonies in South America. A more abundant food supply led to an increase in population. The "population explosion" caused crowded conditions, so some tribes spread south and north in the search for land.

The establishment of British rule in the 1890s marked the beginning of the end for the traditional Zambian kingdoms. But before examining the story of how Zambia became a colony of Great Britain, we must take a closer look at the daily lives of the people when they were still untouched by European culture.

5

Peoples and Traditions

In the traditional societies of Zambia, people followed certain rituals and held certain beliefs that had a great influence on the way they lived. In the Zambian context, "traditional life" refers to how the ancestors of present-day Zambians lived before their customs were affected by constant contact with Europeans. Up until the last two or three decades of the nineteenth century, the peoples of Zambia had such a small amount of exposure to cultures from other continents that their religion, the education of their children, their hunting, fishing, farming, and building methods, and their social relationships were entirely of African origin.

Almost all the Zambian tribes believed in one Supreme Being. However, this God was so distant from the earth that his existence had little meaning. Far more important were the spirits in which the various tribes believed. The Bemba, for example, accredited the power of the Chitimukulu, their chief, to the spirits of his ancestors, who had lived and ruled before him. The spirits of the chiefs, in a sense, had responsibility for the whole tribe and could bring doom to the community, if displeased, or good fortune, if pleased.

The ancestral spirits of each individual had great significance, also. The Tonga called their personal ancestral spirits *mizimu*, and any change in life, such as a move or a journey, had to be announced to one's *mizimu*. A child received the names of certain *mizimu* at birth; these became his guardians, to whom he would have to go for guidance throughout life and from whom he derived his characteristics. Ancestral spirits of chiefs and of individuals were treated with due respect and care was taken not to offend them.

Another type of spirit worship practiced by the Bantu societies and other peoples throughout Africa led to their being called animists. (Sometimes this term refers to ancestral spirit worship as well.) An animist is one who has faith in forces which dwell within objects in nature. These nonpersonal spirits of the Bemba, referred to as *ngulu,* inhabited certain waterfalls, rocks, and other homes in nature. It is important to understand that the Africans did not worship the tree or the rock, but the spirit housed there. The types of spirits worshipped by the peoples of Zambia varied with the needs of each society. All spirits had one common feature, however: the power to intervene in life to promote good or punish evil.

Spirit worship served many purposes. It helped explain unknowns and gave the worshipper some sense of control over them. Personal spirits played a part in defining an individual's role in his society. The Zambians' traditional religion also promoted social stability. They believed change would be an affront to their gods. Witchcraft, sorcery, and a firm belief in the power of magic served the same ends.

The Bemba made a distinction, common to many tribes but not all, between sorcerers and witch doctors. The sorcerer was the person who used magic to bring harm to others. The witch doctor, on the other hand, practiced good magic. He had the power and the medicines to cure illness, to explain why a calamity had occurred, and to provide countermagic that could protect against the sorcerer's spells. The witch doctor also supplied potions for success in love or war. Frequently a witch doctor was an experienced herbalist and had a high degree of success in curing physical ailments.

Another function of the witch doctor was to determine guilt by some sort of ordeal. Instead of a trial, a person suspected of an act such as murder, or of being a sorcerer, might be given poison. If he lived, he was innocent; but if he died, then obviously he was guilty. It might be startling to some Americans to remember that our New England ancestors hunted and condemned witches by equally arbitrary methods.

If a person committed a crime against someone in his own group or village, he would be held personally responsible. However, if he carried it out against someone in another group, his entire village would be blamed and often punished by an attack.

This custom of communal blame and punishment illustrates an important principle among traditional African societies. Whatever a person did or said or believed during his life, good or bad, reflected on the group to which he belonged. Individual values or competitiveness were not only discouraged; they were forbidden. Cooperation with one's neighbors was considered the highest good. In like manner, there was no such thing as private ownership of property. The land was simply in the domain of the tribe that occupied it. Not even the tribe, and certainly no one person, owned any of it. These values conflicted directly with the premium placed on individual initiative by the Europeans who came to live in Zambia.

In traditional societies, children of both sexes were expected to learn the skills of their parents and the mores of their society at a very early age. One way societal values were passed on was through the telling of tales. Historical myths have already been discussed. Another sort of traditional story that is now a part of both African and American cultures is the animal trickster tale. Brer Rabbit of the Uncle Remus stories is familiar to all of us. In Zambia, Brer Rabbit is called Kalulu, the hare. In a Zambian story very similar to that of the Tar Baby, Kalulu becomes mired in sweet gum spread over a tortoise's body. He convinces his captors—in this case an elephant, a hyena, and a lion rather than Brer Fox and Brer Bear—to kill him properly. "I don't ask for kindness. But if you throw me on the hard ground or against a stone I shall live forever. If you drop me on those ashes I shall die at once." * Of course, Kalulu picks himself up from the ashes and runs off into the forest laughing. The trickster tales serve to reassure the hearer that wisdom can triumph over strength, and

* Kay Leitner, *Legends from Zambia* (London: Macmillan Education Ltd., 1971).

that one does have a chance to control powers which at first seem irresistible.

Childhood in Zambia was not the long-drawn-out process that it is in places with many years of formal education. Although very young children were pampered and kept close to their mothers, often tied to their backs until another little one arrived, assumption of adult duties might start as early as seven or eight. Both boys and girls were thought to be capable of and ready for all the responsibilities of adulthood when they reached the age of puberty.

In many African societies, both males and females went through rigorous puberty rites, although in some cases this custom was reserved for only one sex. With or without ceremony, near the time of puberty, or before, males were frequently segregated from their mothers and sisters; in Tonga society, for instance, the boys moved into a separate house between the ages of ten and twelve but there was no accompanying ritual. Both the Bemba and the Lozi had a ceremony for girls that lasted for two or three months.

The Bemba female initiation ceremony was known as the *chisungu*. Often a girl was betrothed, with the exchange of presents between families, in childhood. However, it was thought that she had to be initiated into womanhood before she could be a proper wife. The women of a village would spend many days instructing a young girl in her responsibilities to both her husband and her society. They would attempt to instill in her the tribal attitudes toward sex, fertility, marriage, the rearing of children, as well as a knowledge of political and economic values. Tribal secrets were often revealed at this time. The Bemba were extremely proud of their past and used the initiation rites as a means to pass on their traditions and to keep them alive.

Initiation ceremonies for boys frequently included circumcision, as they did sometimes for girls. Among the Lunda, boys were initiated as a group although girls, as with the Bemba, were instructed individually. The men emphasized hunting, fighting, learning the signals of nature, and tribal lore. The male initiation ceremony of several of Zambia's smaller tribes, the Mbunda,

Luvale, Chokwe, and Luchazi of Western and Northwestern provinces, centered around an elaborate dance known as the *Makishi*. The dancers represented ancestral spirits instructing the initiates. Preparation for marriage was more important for girls, who usually married just after the ceremony, than for boys, who sometimes remained single until their twenties.

A custom associated with marriage was that of *lobola* or bride-price. The contents of the lobola, which a man paid to his wife's father, differed from tribe to tribe. Cattle was the most common payment, but for peoples like the Bemba, who were not herds-men, it often consisted of a period of service by the son-in-law rather than the actual transfer of goods.

Makishi characters during initiation ceremony. From left: Iambunda, a wise old chieftainess; Nalindele, the spirit of a falcon; Chikuza, the stern chief; Kandanji, one of the young initiates; Chizaluke, a wise chief; Likishi lya mwana pwevo, a man dressed as a woman; another Kandanji; Ndondo, a lustful young man.

The new husband paid the lobola at different times in different societies: sometimes at the wedding, but frequently at least partial payment was withheld until after the birth of the first child, as traditional societies considered fertility very important. Failure to have a child was attributed to the woman. In case of a divorce, part of the lobola was sometimes returned.

The bride-price did not mean that a man purchased a wife. A better explanation of its significance is that, just as a marriage license is today, it was the legal or binding part of a marriage. And, even more important, it was the symbol of the joining of two kinship groups.

As strange as it may seem to most Americans, who see marriage in terms of romantic love, the purpose of the African marriage was, above all else, to insure additions to one's kinship group and to provide for children. (A great taboo was placed on the conceiving of children outside of marriage in many tribes.) Marriages were supposedly, although not actually, arranged with no knowledge on the part of the woman. Love was seen as the result of a successful marriage and not as the basis for it. To be a good marriage partner was important because, it was believed by some tribes, unfaithfulness could affect the health of one's spouse.

Marriage ceremonies took many different forms with varying rituals. The Lozi partners, for example, ate porridge off a stone to express the hope that their marriage would be strong and endure. Sometimes there was no single ceremony to begin the marriage; rather there was a long sequence of events.

Among the Ngoni a man was never supposed to speak directly to or even come face to face with his prospective mother-in-law. He was obliged to turn and walk the other way if ever he should see her approaching. Only after the marriage had taken place and was considered successful was there an elaborate ceremony to introduce the husband to the wife's mother.

Polygamy was practiced by most Zambian tribes, but it was not a common occurrence. Only a man with substantial wealth could afford to support more than one wife. Thus, it was more usual for a chief than for a commoner to have several spouses. Paramount chiefs sometimes had fifty to seventy wives. It was not un-usual for a married man to marry his brother's widow when his brother died. Having more than one wife added to one's status.

Ceremonies attended not only puberty and marriage but also death. Many peoples believed that no one died of natural causes but always because he had committed an evil deed or someone else had done evil toward him. Thus, part of the ceremony might be directed to determining guilt. Funerals were long and elaborate. Among the Bemba, old women acted as semipro-fessional mourners. They would wail in loud tones for many hours. Among the Ngoni and other cattle-keeping peoples, a fu-neral was one of the rare occasions when a cow would be killed and eaten. A funeral was thus very special. Cattle were an impor-tant sign of wealth in Bantu societies. A man's prestige rose with the number of cattle he owned.

The structure of kinship groups and family ties was an impor-tant element in traditional societies. In many communities, all one's male relatives were called "father" or "brother" and one's female relatives "mother" or "sister." Members of a clan rarely fought one another and were ready to aid any other clansman who was in need.

Tracing lineage in any of the Zambian societies was a complex process, but a highly symbolic and significant one to an individ-ual. Most of the tribes, except for the Ngoni, are what is known as matrilineal. This means that a man traces his ancestors through his mother, rather than his father, and that often he goes to live with his wife's family after marriage. Children of a widowed father go to the wife's relatives. The matrilineal socie-ties originated with the idea that a baby is given his mother's blood, so that all blood relationships are through her. In this sense, women were much respected.

In some ways, however, African men, especially during lulls in tribal warfare, led a more relaxed and prestigious life than their wives, who were far from liberated. Men very seldom associated with women socially. Companionship was not thought of as a part of marriage. The women had their tasks and interests and the men had theirs. In addition to gardening and cooking and caring for the children, the women were expected to bear most heavy burdens. The African women became extremely skilled at carrying great loads in delicate balance on their heads. Beer brewing, pottery making, basket weaving, and the making of clothes were also tasks for the women.

The men, in addition to hunting and fighting, fished. The Lozi alone developed twenty-two different methods of trapping fish. The males also performed most of the ceremonial dances, made weapons, gathered the heaviest wood, and built huts.

Huts rarely lasted more than five or six years, so construction was a fairly frequent and time-consuming task. The traditional Zambian hut was round. Originally dwellings were built by plac-

Zambian women at work.

ing wooden poles of the appropriate size in a circle and then covering the structure with grass or straw. Later—no one is sure exactly when—mud came into use to reinforce the walls and only the roofs were thatched. The huts were small and frequently had no windows.

In precolonial Zambia, the concept of a house was not the same as it is today. Instead of several rooms, a traditional house consisted of only one small room, but numerous huts, each with a distinct purpose, were often grouped together and used by a single family unit. The number of huts depended on the size of the family and the various types of shelters they needed. One family's living quarters might consist of two huts for wives, a children's sleeping hut, a men's shelter, a kitchen, a spirit hut, a latrine, several food storage bins, and a chicken coop. Not all families had such an elaborate arrangement. Sometimes a specific type of structure, such as a kitchen or a pantry, would be shared. Usually there were one or two cattle kraals per village.

Huts in the traditional village were usually grouped around a kraal or around the chief's compound. Sometimes they were in a circle with the shared structures around the edges.

The arrival of foreigners started a process of change in traditional societies, sometimes drastic, sometimes barely noticeable. Today there are few, if any, places in Zambia where life is lived exactly as it was before the events of the past one hundred years.

6

Slavers, Explorers, Missionaries

The exploration of Africa by people from other continents was a slow process, strung out over many centuries. It occurred in the pattern of a cookie being nibbled around the outer edges with the center part saved for the last. Since Zambia lies far to the interior of Africa, other peoples reached it later than they did the coastal areas.

Arabs began sailing their dhows down the east coast of Africa from Saudi Arabia before the birth of Christ. After the death of Mohammed in the seventh century A.D., Arabs set off to gain converts to Islam, and their settlements on the African coast multiplied. Slavery had long been a part of life in Arabia, and Africa soon became the chief source of supply for these slaves. Arab slave traders were active at Ingombe Ilede in southern Zambia over one thousand years ago. The Arabs, however, did not penetrate deep into Zambia until the approach of the nineteenth century.

The first Europeans to reach Zambia were the Portuguese, who arrived in the early eighteenth century. Three hundred years before, the Portuguese had begun their great age of exploration along the coastlines of Africa. The long-range goal of all Portuguese exploration was to find a sea route to India in order to dominate the spice trade. Vasco da Gama fulfilled this dream in 1498 when he rounded the Cape of Good Hope at the bottom of Africa and sailed up the east coast and on to India.

The Arabs, after seven centuries of dominating the east coast of Africa, were at last challenged. Firearms versus swords and bows and arrows made the Portuguese the victors, at least for a while. In 1507 the first white men to settle permanently in Africa landed in Mozambique, but little if any effort was made to reach inward from the shore. Feira, within the borders of present-day Zambia at the convergence of the Zambezi and Luangwa rivers, was founded as a trading post by the Portuguese over two hundred years later. The total number of Portuguese inhabitants of the Mozambique-Zambia territory rarely exceeded one thousand before the twentieth century.

By the mid-eighteenth century, Portuguese traders had penetrated Zambia from the opposite direction as well. The Lunda and the Lozi traded for goods brought in from Angola to the west. With Mozambique to the east and Angola to the west, the Portuguese soon sought a route to link the two. This route, of course, would lie directly across Zambia.

More and more the Portuguese had become identified as cruel and ruthless slavers. The demand for labor grew along with the development of Portugal's New World colony, Brazil. It became increasingly apparent that a route between Mozambique and Angola would greatly increase the efficiency of the slave traffic. Although he knew there was much anti-Portuguese feeling among the Africans, Dr. Francisco Jose Maria de Lacerda decided to attempt a journey from coast to coast. He was a Brazilian who had also served as court astronomer in Lisbon. The government in Portugal enthusiastically backed Lacerda and provided him with means to assemble an expedition consisting of over 450 persons, many of whom were slaves.

The procession entered Zambia from Mozambique in the southeast on September 21, 1798, and turned northward. But the barriers to success were too high, the slave porters mutinied, and the journey ended at the court of the Kazembe of the Lunda in northern Zambia. Lacerda died there of malaria. No one had the courage to risk the remaining one thousand miles without a leader.

Seven years after Lacerda died, two half-caste Portuguese, Pedro Joao Battista and Amaro Jose, journeyed from Angola in the west to the court of the Kazembe, where they were kept prisoner for four years. Finally they were allowed to complete their journey to Tete in the east and became the first men to span the continent. After around 1830, the Portuguese seemed to lose interest in their plan to link their two territories and abandoned further organized attempts until many years later.

The Portuguese explorers kept some written records, but generally they were poorly educated and little trained in the powers of observation. The best of the diaries were not published until nearly seventy-five years after the journeys were made. Thus, this part of Africa remained little known to the rest of the world.

The Arabs and the Portuguese were the first non-Africans to tread on Zambian soil, but the "outsiders" who were to figure most prominently in the history of Zambia were the British. The slave trade was one of the many areas in which British actions affected the course of events in Zambia. By the mid-eighteenth century, before slaving was widespread in Zambia, Great Britain had been recognized as the world leader in the slave trade. Yet, approximately fifty years later, in 1807, the British Parliament outlawed slave trading by British ships, and in 1833 slavery was forbidden in all British possessions. This meant that when Zambia came under British rule, slaving became illegal there also.

But a ban on slavery was not easy to enforce. The ships of Great Britain patrolled the coast of West Africa attempting to put a stop to all the slave carriers. Although on the high seas visible signs of the slave trade decreased due to Britain's vigilance, the slave raids continued and pushed farther into the interior of Africa. Efforts to stop the slave traffic reached the east coast in the 1830s. It was at this time and for the next few decades that the turmoil caused by slave raiders reached a peak in Zambia.

The Arab and Portuguese traders were notorious for their cruelty toward the slaves. Typically, the slave raiders burned villages without thought. Africans were chained together and forced to march to the sea, carrying great burdens, with little food or water. Any sign of weakness was punished by death. Explorers report finding the paths through Zambia littered with skeletons of the sick and weak among the slaves who had been abandoned. The following account was given by Albert J. Swann, a missionary who approached the leader of a caravan to ask about slave women with children. Swann asked, "What do you do in their case when they become too weak to carry both child and ivory? Who carries the ivory?" The answer was, "She does! We cannot leave valuable ivory on the road. We spear the child and make her burden lighter. Ivory first, child afterwards!"

There were six major slave trading routes on the continent of Africa, and two of these led into Zambia. Tall lines of palm trees which the slavers planted to mark their routes can be seen today. One route from the north started at the Arab island of Zanzibar in the Indian Ocean, for many years the largest center of slave

Slavers taking revenge for their losses. From David Livingstone's *Last Journals.*

export in the world, crossed Tanzania, and entered Zambia. Tippoo Tib, the most notorious Arab slaver of all time, reached Zambia by this route. The other route started from the coast in Mozambique and entered Zambia from the south. Slavers also reached Zambia along minor routes through Malawi and Portuguese-controlled Angola. The Portuguese, as allies of England, publicly denounced slavery but privately carried on their business as usual.

One of the worst consequences of the slave trade was the increase of intertribal warfare. The Arabs and the Portuguese frequently did not capture the slaves themselves but traded with the more powerful tribes which had raided the weaker tribes and taken captives. Thus, slavery set tribe against tribe in the most violent warfare in the history of the continent. The Bemba, for example, were active in providing slaves to the Arabs on the northern route. In return, they received guns, with which they could even more easily intimidate and capture weaker peoples. This is not to say that the Bemba, or other tribes which made the decision to trade in human lives, can be completely condemned, because it very soon became evident that the tribes which could obtain European weapons found survival far easier. Both the Ngoni and the Lozi were organized and skillful enough to withstand fairly successfully involvement in the European slave trade.

Sometimes people say the Europeans did not really start slavery in Africa because the Africans themselves kept slaves before the coming of the Europeans. This is true of some tribes. The Lozi had slaves in their own households. There was, however, no buying or selling of human life. The slaves were respected as human beings and were often given the opportunity for freedom.

European slaving brought about drastic and negative changes in Zambia. In some areas, agriculture was almost totally abandoned because of the general unrest and the loss of much of the work force. Also, since the traders were more interested in slaves than in anything the Africans could grow to sell, there was no reason to attempt to expand the crops. Some places became se-

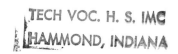

verely depopulated. As the population decreased, slavers pushed farther into the interior. It has been estimated that twenty to thirty thousand slaves were sold annually in the Zanzibar market. For every slave sold, three others were killed in raids or died on the way to the coast.

The man who did the most to tell the rest of the world what was really happening and to speed on correction of the horrors of slavery was the explorer and missionary, David Livingstone. Livingstone was the first Englishman to travel through Zambia. He focused the attention of England on this little-known and less thought of corner of the world.

Livingstone was born in Scotland in 1813. Possibly his greatest quality was his ability to carry on with a task, no matter how difficult, once he felt it was worthwhile.

Livingstone's family was poor and he attended night classes because he had to spend his days working in a spinning factory. His family was devoutly Christian. While at the University of Glasgow, he decided to combine the study of theology with that of medicine in order to become a medical missionary. The London Missionary Society sent him to Africa.

From the beginning Livingstone rebelled at the idea that missionaries should live a comfortable, easy life in the towns. He went first to Kuruman, a mission station in the Republic of South Africa * run by a man named Robert Moffat, whose daughter, Mary, he later married. As soon as he was settled, he pushed farther north, attempting to find a suitable place to establish a mission of his own. Disappointments and failures marred his first efforts, as they did almost all his efforts in life. His original mission station was burned by the Dutch settlers, who wanted no one to disturb the Africans they held as slaves.

After Livingstone's wife and children almost perished crossing the Kalahari Desert, he reluctantly decided they had better return to England. He saw very little of them after that and deeply regretted the suffering he caused them. Yet he was a man who

* In the remainder of this book the name South Africa will refer to the Republic of South Africa.

David Livingstone.

could let nothing, not even his family, stand in the way of his vision for Africa. Mary's death from malaria when she joined David once again on a later journey was one of the personal tragedies most difficult for him to overcome, even though they had been separated for most of their marriage.

In June 1851, at the age of thirty-eight, Livingstone first sighted the Zambezi River, and from then until his death in 1873 he spent most of his time in Zambia. For a long while he saw as his main purpose the marking out of trade routes and paths by which teachers, doctors, and missionaries could reach the interior of the continent. Later his intense geographical curiosity was the main force which urged him on. During his travels through Zambia, Livingstone was not only a medical missionary, but an explorer, a geographer, a botanist, a geologist, and a historian as well.

In 1853, Livingstone and some of the Makololo set out from western Zambia to reach the Atlantic Ocean. After incredible hardships, they arrived at their destination. Rather than sailing to England to report his success, Livingstone insisted on retracing his footsteps with the Makololo to their homes because he had promised to help them return.

Livingstone did not remain in western Zambia. He continued down the Zambezi until, in 1856, he reached the east coast of Africa. He had crossed the continent, not with the grand retinue that Lacerda had had, but with a handful of helpers. His journey opened the door to the unknown heart of Africa, to the country now known as Zambia. It was on this journey that Livingstone came upon the majestic Victoria Falls. It is interesting that this is the only one of Livingstone's "discoveries" to which he gave an English name.

His transcontinental trek was the first of David Livingstone's three great journeys. During this first journey he saw all the horrors caused by the slave trade, and he saw that it was not dying out despite the official ban. He called slavery the "open sore of the world" and said the men who were enslaved died of "the strange disease of broken-heartedness." He became consumed with a desire to stop the trade somehow.

Livingstone believed that if Europeans would come into Africa and teach the Africans how to engage in trade and commerce in order to obtain what they wanted, there would no longer be the incentive for tribesman to turn against tribesman. He tried to encourage as many people as possible to go to Africa. Sometimes, perhaps unintentionally, he made life there seem less harsh than it really was. The first missionaries to respond to his call to Zambia arrived with their families. All who came were stricken with illness and died almost immediately.

As part of his attempt to interest Europeans in coming to Zambia, Livingstone wrote two books. The first, published in England in 1857, *Missionary Travel and Researches in South Africa,* was an instant best-seller, as was his second, *Narrative of an Expedition to the Zambezi and its Tributaries.*

Livingstone went to England in 1856. When he returned to

Baines and Chapman, Englishmen who accompanied Livingstone. Sketch by Baines.

Africa, he was sent out by the British government rather than by a missionary society. His second journey, from 1859 to 1864, was intended to open a trade route up the Zambezi. This was the only journey on which other Englishmen accompanied him. With him went an artist, Thomas Baines, a botanist, and other specialists. The trip was a disaster, both because Livingstone turned out to be too strong a personality to work successfully with other men and because the Zambezi proved to be unnavigable.

Livingstone's final journey, from 1866 to 1873, left him in deep despair. His dreams were beginning to wear thin. He found that the trails he had opened were used by slave raiders, who even called themselves "Livingstone's children." He had hoped to find the source of the Nile, but was too far south, although his wanderings did provide valuable information on the Congo River system. His medicine chest was stolen, so he had no way to treat or prevent malaria or dysentery. The East Indians he had hired to go with him deserted and spread the rumor that he had been killed. This was later disproved but eventually led Henry Morton Stanley to make his famous trip to find the explorer. Probably the most remembered and least important thing about Livingstone is the remark Stanley made to him, "Dr. Livingstone, I presume." Saddest of all was that Livingstone had to depend, during the last years of his life, on the Arabs, whose actions he detested so much, because they were the only people who reached the interior of Africa with supplies.

He died in Zambia near Lake Bangweulu on May 1, 1873, as he knelt in prayer by his bed. He had covered over thirty thousand miles on foot.

Livingstone is best known as an explorer, but his work as a missionary also had a lasting effect. Although he never established a permanent mission and left few, if any, firm converts to Christianity, he provided the opportunity for others to do so. He broadened the concept of missionary responsibility to include not only religious instruction but also medical care, the teaching of farming methods, and general aid to the well-being of the Africans. He drove the Africans who worked with him to be as dedicated to his ideals as he was himself. At times he was impatient, but he was never cruel, and his memory is honored among Zambians. The town of Livingstone in southern Zambia is the only Zambian town or city that has not changed its name from a European to an African one since Independence.

In May 1973, many services and other special events were held in Zambia to commemorate the centenary of the death of Dr. Livingstone. President Kaunda conducted a ceremony at Chitambo's Village, now known as Chipundu, where Livingstone died. Mainza Chona, then the vice-president, addressed a rally at Ndola. There are few explorers who are praised and revered in this manner by Africans of any nation.

Livingstone, however, is not without his critics. The hundredth anniversary of his death was also marked by the publication of a very uncomplimentary biography, written by a British novelist, Tim Jeal. At the same time that he helped bring an end to the slave trade, Livingstone encouraged and believed in the colonialism (the control of Africa by Britain) that brought much grief in later years. Personally, Livingstone was egotistical and could not allow himself to be bettered by others, nor could he work cooperatively with any other white man. Moreover, Jeal accuses Livingstone of working with Africans because he could dominate them. It is only fair to be aware of both the strengths and weaknesses of Livingstone and to realize that there were both positive and negative aspects of his work.

Missionary activity greatly increased after the death of Livingstone. The first missionaries in southern Africa had been Roman Catholic, particularly Jesuit. It was only in the nineteenth century that Protestant missionaries began to arrive. Gradually, different missionary groups "staked a claim" to certain parts of Zambia. It was easier for one group to work in an area where most of the people spoke the same language.

The wave of missionaries who arrived in the last decades of the nineteenth century came with a zeal to put a stop to slavery. Livingstone had brought to everyone's attention the fact that slavery simply had not ceased.

European nations used the desire to put an end to slavery to conceal other, more selfish motives as they moved in and formally declared themselves rulers of tropical Africa. In the last two decades of the nineteenth century, a series of conferences was held and agreements were signed, carefully designating which territory belonged to which nation. Although Portugal made a last-minute attempt to claim the central part of Africa between her recognized colonies of Angola and Mozambique, she had neglected her opportunity too long, and the territory that would one day become Zambia fell into the laps of the British.

7

The Seeds of Discontent

As the colonial power in charge of the territory, Great Britain had the responsibility of stopping the slave trade and of bringing peace north of the Zambezi. Before the large copper deposits were discovered, the effort to govern this area hardly seemed worthwhile. Except, that is, to Cecil John Rhodes, the man for whom Northern and Southern Rhodesia were named.

Cecil Rhodes had come to South Africa in 1870 at the age of seventeen in search of warmth and wealth. He found both. By the age of twenty-four, Rhodes had formulated a grandiose plan to extend the British empire, and thus "civilization," to all of Africa. He saw the land north of the Zambezi as an important part of his scheme. The government in Britain was only too glad to hand over to him the task of settling the area.

Rhodes was economically and politically in a position to carry out his plans. By 1880, at the age of twenty-seven, he had become a millionaire in the South African diamond mines. He then entered politics and, in 1890, was elected prime minister of Cape Colony of South Africa. He decided to invest his resources and persuaded others to join him in forming the British South Africa Company (BSAC). From Britain, he obtained a charter that gave the company power to govern. For the last decade of the nineteenth century and the first two of the twentieth century, Zambia was ruled not by another country, but by a company.

Rhodes sent representatives of the BSAC to make treaties with the chiefs to the north. The treaties were deceitful in several ways. The chiefs who signed thought they would be protected from other tribes, from slavers, or any threats whatever, by the British government. Much was made of allegiance to the "Great White Queen." But when they needed help, they had only the BSAC to turn to. Secondly, the chiefs were promised many items, including weapons and money, most of which they never received. Finally, the chiefs understood that the British were to use the land rather than to own it permanently; in the African culture, land was never to be bought or sold but simply held in trust for whoever would use it next.

Several men stand out in the history of Northern Rhodesia as "concession hunters," the rugged individuals who were sent to make the treaties. To Barotseland, where the Lozi (sometimes called the Barotse) lived, went Frank Lochner. Zambia's best-known missionary, François Coillard, was already established there. For many months, the two men worked together in persuading the powerful King Lewanika to sign a treaty, which extended British influence to the northern boundaries of present-day Zambia and to the Kafue River in the east.

With an elaborate ceremony, the treaty was signed in June 1890. The treaty included rights to the as yet unknown Copperbelt. In the years to come, there was much dispute over whether this part of the agreement was legal, since the Lozi did not actually rule the Lamba tribe, who at that time lived on the Copperbelt.

Lewanika immediately regretted his decision. But through this treaty and later ones, he retained for himself and the Lozi much more control than the BSAC allowed any other of the Northern Rhodesian peoples. The Lozi always saw themselves as a "colony within a colony." This led to problems when Zambia gained independence, because the Lozi claimed to be a separate nation.

In 1899, the territory covered by these treaties became known as North-West Rhodesia. In the same year, the eastern wing of the Zambian butterfly became North-Eastern Rhodesia. Harry Johnston, Alfred Sharpe, and Joseph Thomson were the company's concession hunters here. Thomson alone negotiated more than fourteen treaties with chiefs, covering forty thousand square miles of territory.

Lochner (left) and King Lewanika (right) discuss treaty as people in background give royal salute. Engraving from photograph taken by Coillard.

Things were not to go so smoothly in this part of Zambia, however. The Bemba, the Lunda, and the Ngoni refused to accept British authority. Here the situation was, for a short time, like that in the old American West in that force was used to subdue the people of the land. The Arab slave traders, as well as the Africans, resisted occupation. Johnston built a number of forts and fought the slave raiders. British troops came in from neighboring Nyasaland to crush uprisings of the tribes. By the end of the century the area was peaceful and the slave trade had stopped.

The beginning years of the twentieth century marked a new phase of missionary activity. Nearly every group had founded at least one mission in the area which would "belong" to it. The different "brands" of Christianity and the rivalry among them puzzled the Africans. During the next twenty years the mission stations were expanded. Often, large villages grew up around them. The occupants of these villages were almost exclusively Christian converts. Converts settled in mission villages because the missionaries rewarded them with employment. Other Africans were welcomed less and less as the years went by.

By 1924, there were over one hundred thousand Northern Rhodesians who professed to be Christians, but no one knows exactly what standard was used to determine who was and was not converted or how lasting the conversions were. The largest group of Christians, approximately one-fourth of the total, were Catholic. The others were split among the various Protestant denominations.

Most of the missionaries came with the best of intentions, but they failed, for the most part, to understand or see any value in the Africans' own culture. Moreover, their initial impressions of the Africans were frequently very negative. This was partly because they arrived at a time when the land was torn apart by the slave trade and the people were afflicted with severe malnutrition as a result of the disruption of agriculture.

The Africans showed little interest in the missionaries' teachings. Their education began with memorizing the European alphabet and Bible verses. To most Africans it made little sense to waste time in learning either. They were taught the history and civilization of Europe and were led to believe that their own history was not worth learning. Their lack of interest in these subjects was seen by the missionaries as a sign of laziness, as was their evident unwillingness to strive to better themselves. The African tradition of cooperation, according to which no one was supposed to make himself seem better than anyone else, conflicted with the European notion of individual achievement.

Reports sent home by the early missionaries stated that the Africans were immoral as well as unindustrious. The missionaries made the mistake of equating the message of Christianity with the morality and mores of Western Europe. Unsuccessfully, they tried to persuade chiefs that it was wrong to have more than one wife. The Africans could not understand why a loving God would demand that they give up their most sacred customs. Equally offensive to the missionaries was the Africans' unwillingness to adopt European-style clothing. This was a sin equal to witchcraft and polygamy in the minds of most missionaries.

Despite their misguided plans and methods, many missionaries had a positive and lasting effect on the lives of the Africans whom they served. A number of Africa's first national leaders, including Kenneth Kaunda of Zambia, received their education at mission stations. New techniques of farming and principles of health care helped a people devastated by slavery begin to recover.

Also significant was the missionaries' defense of the Africans' right to stay on the land where they had always lived. This became necessary because of the arrival of another group of "outsiders," the settlers. The BSAC offered incentives to Europeans settled in South Africa to move farther north to the newly secured territories. Many Europeans poured into Southern Rhodesia. Fewer people made it across the Zambezi, as the opportunities there seemed slim. Malaria mosquitoes and tsetse flies were a serious hazard to health. It took a real pioneer spirit to push farther north. Although most settlers came from the south, some moved into Northern Rhodesia from the east.

The first settlers staked their claims along the line-of-rail, in the north beside Lake Tanganyika, and in the Eastern Province. There were prospectors and traders, but the largest group were the cotton and tobacco farmers near Fort Jameson close to the Nyasaland border. This was one of the few overpopulated areas of Northern Rhodesia, and the Europeans soon began to make demands that the Africans move and leave the land for them.

The idea of land "reserved" for use by one race alone began to take hold. In 1907, the first reservation was marked off in the land of the Ngoni. The plan was very similar to reservations for North American Indians. At this time, Africans had to move onto a reserve only if they chose to.

Later, in the 1920s, Native Reserves became a policy of the British government. Africans could be notified and had to move from their villages within a year. New villages could not be started outside the reserve areas without the governor's consent. While most of the land was marked either for reserves or for "native trust" land (to be used as needed), the richest and best land was kept for the Europeans.

The Africans have a saying which is basically true: "When the whites came to our country, we had the land and they had the Bible. Now we have the Bible and they have the land." Crowding of Africans into the designated lands caused widespread hunger and discontent. The missionaries violently opposed this system, which laid foundations for an apartheid type of society. Apartheid amounts to strict separation of the races, with the Africans always receiving the poorest part of the bargain. Luckily, the reserve system was never fully developed in Northern Rhodesia.

Unfortunately, the missionaries did not oppose and, in fact, were partly responsible for two taxes that altered traditional society more than anything else imposed by the Europeans. The first was the hut tax, a tax on each dwelling a person built. Later, a poll tax was imposed. After a village was "polled," or counted, a tax was collected according to the number of residents.

The government and the missionaries were in favor of these taxes because they needed the Africans as cheap labor. Since the Africans had no means to earn the cash needed for the tax except by working for the Europeans, a ready labor force was created. In order to earn money, many Northern Rhodesians were forced to migrate to other countries, especially those to the south, to work in mines or on plantations. By 1936, approximately sixty thousand Northern Rhodesian males were employed in other countries. Few men were left behind in villages, and the already poor agriculture suffered even more. The disruption of family and tribal life was overwhelming. In some West African colonies there were actual wars to protest the taxes. In Northern Rhodesia, the Africans protested, but less violently.

Cecil Rhodes had died in 1902. During the next two decades the BSAC became weary of the expense of managing the territory north of the Zambezi. The settlers disliked the company's strict policies regarding mineral and land rights and were especially displeased with an income tax imposed on them in 1920. So, in 1924, the BSAC ceased its rule and Northern Rhodesia came directly under the wing of Great Britain. (In 1911, North-Eastern Rhodesia and North-West Rhodesia had been united to form the colony of Northern Rhodesia, with the capital at Livingstone.)

Almost as an afterthought, the BSAC demanded the right to royalties from any mineral deposits found in North-West Rhodesia. This was to prove a curse to the colony until Independence. An enormous share of the revenue was shipped off to the BSAC. In 1939, the BSAC drew as much money in copper royalties as the Northern Rhodesian government got from copper taxes. This arrangement, of course, took away money that could have been used to develop health, education, and other programs in Northern Rhodesia.

As a colony, Northern Rhodesia was ruled by a governor appointed from Britain. There was also an executive council of senior government officials and a legislative council with nine appointed members and five elected members. The rules for voting were arranged so that few, if any, Africans could vote; thus, the elected members were sure to be white. A province commissioner administered each of the eight provinces. Each province was broken into smaller districts served by district commissioners.

Many of the colonial officials went to great lengths to make themselves feel at home. One district commissioner built an English-style castle on a remote hillside of the Eastern Province. Today, the castle serves as a government rest house.

Great Britain never figured out how to involve the local people in government without giving them too much power. The official British policy was to work through chiefs. This was known as "indirect rule." The Native Authorities Act of 1929 made the rural chiefs an official part of the government. It did not work, for several reasons. The Tonga, for instance, had never had chiefs, so the British created them. Naturally, the people had no reason to respect such chiefs. With so much of the population moving around seeking employment and with the days of tribal warfare at an end, even the traditional chiefs lost much of their authority.

The opening of the Copperbelt in the late 1920s brought a large wave of Europeans to work in the mines. Most of them came from either South Africa or England. By 1930, there were over four thousand whites on the Copperbelt, as many as had been in the entire country in 1921.

This great influx of white men marked the beginning of a period of severe racial discrimination against the Africans. Discrimination had existed before, but urbanization led to legislation designed to maintain racial separation in the more densely populated areas. African housing in the cities was poor and always strictly segregated from the spacious and expensive dwellings of the Europeans. In Livingstone, it was against the law for a black

Housing provided for the Africans by the mining companies.

person to walk on the pavement, and in one month over forty-three people were arrested for this offense. Africans were not allowed to enter theaters or restaurants. Many storekeepers refused to serve Africans. Those who did sell to Africans made them wait until all Europeans had been waited on. Africans were required to have special passes or permits to travel, and in some cases in order to receive visitors or to be outside at night. Especially difficult for the African to understand was the discrimination in the churches. The Africans were expected to attend churches created by the missionaries just for them, with the finer buildings reserved for whites.

Taunts were shouted at the Africans, such as "boy," "nigger," or "kaffir," a South African word equivalent to "nigger." The man who was to become president of Zambia once encountered a district commissioner who refused to speak to him in English because only African languages were good enough for so-called savages. Prejudice extended all the way to the animal kingdom. On the metal tags that dogs wore around their necks was stamped either "European dog" or "African dog."

Wage and job discrimination were equally bad. In 1940, a white truck driver was paid ten times more than an African for doing exactly the same job. Wages for an identical task were frequently fifteen to twenty times more for a white person. Even worse, there was no provision for Africans to advance. A European, A. M. Alexander, writing in the 1920s, maintained that Africans should be lifted "a little bit above the primitive," but one must be careful because "to teach motor driving and so on would be wrong. . . . What would become of the white children when they grew up?" The British and the mine officials encouraged Africans to work only a couple of years in the mines and then to return to their home villages. In this way, no African would become skilled enough to demand a higher job.

In short, the Europeans were, indeed, bringing "civilization" as they saw it, but they were reserving the best parts of it for themselves.

The seeds of discontent were sown. Everywhere the African looked he was oppressed in his native land. The white settlers also were discontented; they wanted to gain more control from the officials sent out from Great Britain. At this point, it was unclear whether the whites would triumph and would have absolute control in Northern Rhodesia as they eventually did in Southern Rhodesia and South Africa, or whether the Africans could gain the strength and unity to steer their own course and determine their own future.

8

Federation and Freedom

During the early years of British occupation, the Africans protested little against the discrimination and the disruption of their lives. Some of the smaller tribes even felt more secure for a time, as they were protected from raids by their larger and more powerful neighbors. But this soon proved a false security, for they were raided in a different manner. The Europeans were gradually stripping them of any power over their own lives and were giving them little to replace the pride they once had had in tribal heritage and traditions.

Several important things caused the seeds of discontent to sprout in the minds of the Africans and take root. One was the active role Africans played in World War II. During the war, they were sent wherever British troops were in battle. After fighting as equals side by side with white men, it was difficult for the Africans to return to the unequal conditions of daily life in their own country. During the war, many Africans began to think of Northern Rhodesia as a nation, their nation, for the first time.

Another group of Africans, workers returning from the mines in Southern Rhodesia and South Africa, found conditions for Africans much less oppressive in Northern Rhodesia than in the countries to the south. But they feared that Northern Rhodesia was moving in the direction of her southern neighbors and desperately wanted to stop the process before it was too late.

Finally, a growing group of mission-educated Africans gave the Northern Rhodesians a set of leaders who understood the ways of the Europeans and could deal with them on their own terms.

In the beginning, of course, the Africans were moved not to struggle for independence but rather for better treatment and opportunities in general. Very slowly, Africans who opposed the way things were began to organize. The original organizations were called "welfare societies," and this is exactly what they were: groups formed to promote the well-being of Africans. In 1923, the first welfare society was formed at Mwenzo in the Northern Province. One of the four founders was David Kaunda, the father of Zambia's first president. One activity of the association was a protest against the poll tax. Other rural welfare societies of the 1920s were purely social groups concerned with arranging weddings, funerals, and similar occasions. However, in 1930, several societies were founded along the line-of-rail, and these were definitely political.

In 1933, there was an attempt to establish a United African Welfare Association, but it was not until 1946 that the welfare societies successfully joined together to form the Northern Rhodesian Federation of Welfare Societies. The joining together of the local groups was a step toward the formation of an African political party.

During this time, Africans were also forming unions. The first allowed by the British was on the Copperbelt in 1935. The unions were a strong force in attempting to gain better working conditions and more rights for Africans on the job. Individual union members supported the political activities of other African groups, but the unions as a whole did not become actively involved in politics until victory for the Africans was certain. For the members, the job risk was too crucial.

Meanwhile, the British were making some attempts to further include Africans in the process of ruling, but always as advisors, never with any actual power. Urban advisory councils were set up as early as 1938 to allow the Africans in the cities to express their views as the rural Africans did through the native authorities (chiefs). Building on these two structures, the British organized provincial councils, bringing together rural and urban Af-

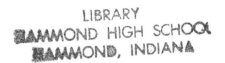

ricans as well as some representatives from the welfare societies. Finally, the African Representative Council was created at the national level, drawing from these more local groups.

It was also in 1938 that the African point of view was first represented in the Legislative Council. An aristocratic European farmer, Sir Stewart Gore-Brown, was appointed to speak for African interests. He held this position for many years. Except for the period during which he campaigned for Northern Rhodesia to join with the south, he was looked upon as a fair champion of African rights. In 1948, the first African, Nelson Nalumango, was elected to the council.

The Northern Rhodesian Africans soon realized that the organizations and representations set up for them by Europeans were giving them no real power. Many Europeans had believed that the Africans would be content to meet occasionally and simply debate issues affecting them. They were not. So, in 1948, what had been the Northern Rhodesian Federation of Welfare Societies changed its name and its stated purposes and became the Northern Rhodesia African Congress, a political party started by and for Africans.

Leaders of the white opposition were emerging as the Africans gained influence. In 1941, Roy Welensky, a railwayman, established a Labour party for Europeans. He remained at the forefront of the fight for white supremacy until the day of Zambia's independence. He emphatically stated, "I will never accept that Northern Rhodesia is to be an African state," and that, "If the British government wants to implement it [independence], it will have to bring troops to this country." He declared that for Africans to have the right to vote was "rubbish and completely unsuitable."

By 1951, Harry Nkumbula had become the leader of the Africans and president of the Northern Rhodesia African National Congress (ANC), as it was now known. Nkumbula was a teacher from the Southern Province who had graduated from Makerere College in Uganda and had been sent for further study in London.

During the early 1950s, three distinct groups were involved in shaping the course Northern Rhodesia was to take. The white settlers, including Gore-Brown and Welensky, although they differed on their attitudes toward Africans, agreed that the settlers should gain control of the colony. The Africans were becoming more and more politically aware. The British government had begun to look for some way to please everyone and be relieved of responsibilty.

From the early 1920s, the white population had been mildly interested in a union of some kind with Southern Rhodesia. Since 1925, the whites of Southern Rhodesia had run a self-governing colony. The British had never considered Southern Rhodesia a protectorate for Africans as they did Northern Rhodesia. More whites had settled south of the Zambezi than in the north. This had laid the foundation for the extreme difference between the policies for the two colonies.

The Northern Rhodesians held back from a union because they did not relish the thought of sharing their wealth, and because they feared losing control to the south. However, in the early 1950s, unrest in other colonies, especially in Kenya, made the whites of Northern Rhodesia uneasy and more anxious to join forces with the whites in the south. At first, the whites of Southern Rhodesia saw no advantage to joining with the poorer, less-developed country to the north, but after the boom of copper in the 1940s, the benefits became very clear indeed.

Throughout the years, many plans had been set forth for uniting not only Northern and Southern Rhodesia but Nyasaland, to the east, as well. After over twenty-five years of consideration, the decision was finally reached in 1952 to join the three colonies in the Central African Federation. Europeans in all three colonies could now see advantages to be gained. The economic advantages of the Federation were the main reason Great Britain gave for its existence. In the eyes of the Africans, it was nothing more than a step by the whites to assure themselves of eventual and long-lasting power. Other British colonies had come together in a federation and eventually had gained independence as a unit, for example Canada and Australia. If Great Britain would recognize the independence of the white-controlled Federation and thus legitimize white dominance in the eyes of the world, the chances for African rule would be greatly reduced.

The scheme for the Federation was put to a vote in the three colonies. In Northern Rhodesia, the Africans in the Legislative Council, as well as those Europeans representing African interests, voted against it. The ANC campaigned vigorously against federation. All the leaders of the Congress, including Kenneth Kaunda, who had been elected secretary-general of the ANC, violently opposed the plan. Harry Nkumbula called for a "national day of prayer" on the date set for the Federation to begin. Africans were asked to go on strike. The mine officials and other employers got word of the strike and threatened their employees with immediate dismissal should they participate, so the protest did not succeed. The Federation came into being on October 23, 1953.

The federal government took responsibility for defense, communications, European agriculture, and European education. The governments of the three territories had power for all African affairs including agriculture, education, housing, and roads. A federal legislature of thirty-five members was set up, but the majority of the members were from Southern Rhodesia and by law only six were African.

The first five years of the Federation were peaceful and seemingly properous. Foreign investors had confidence in the union and a number of new projects were funded. "Partnership" was the word stressed everywhere. Sitting in Lusaka during the days of federation was a statue of a horse and rider. To the Africans it represented the type of partnership that existed in the Federation: the European rider as partner of his horse, the African, who must serve him. Kenneth Kaunda hated this statue and had it removed as soon as he became Zambia's president.

By the end of 1959, the Federation was doomed, although it did not break apart until 1963. Not only the blacks, but many of the whites of Northern Rhodesia had become extremely dissatisfied with the arrangement.

It became more and more clear that Southern Rhodesia was

receiving the most benefits from the Federation. The Federation's capital was Salisbury in Southern Rhodesia. The Africans began to call Salisbury *Bamba Zonke* which means "take-all." It has been estimated that during the ten years of federation over $210 million was taken from Northern Rhodesia and spent for the benefit of the Europeans in Southern Rhodesia. In 1956, Sir Roy Welensky became head of the federal government. Although he was a Northern Rhodesian, his sympathies were very much with the colony to the south.

A blatant example of southern dominance, and a situation that contributed to the breakup of the Federation, was a decision to halt work on a dam at Kafue in Northern Rhodesia and to transfer the hydroelectric project to Kariba on the Zambezi. Arguments for the move were that the dam would be more centrally located, that it would be larger and could supply an enormous amount of power, and that the existence of such an impressive project would increase the support of foreign investors and generally help the economy of the Federation. Little attention was paid to the drastically needed irrigation project that had been planned to help Northern Rhodesia at Kafue.

Kariba was a grander scheme, but it turned out to be much too big. The development was planned for several stages, yet the power output of the first stage has never been fully used. Twice during construction costly repairs have been required because floods weakened the dam's foundations. The worse problem for Northern Rhodesia was that the only power station was on the southern side of the dam. This gave Southern Rhodesia a threat to hold over the head of Northern Rhodesia, because the south controlled the power supply for both countries.

It was not until federation that the mass of the African people started thinking seriously of independence. Many Northern Rhodesian whites had hoped that joining with white-dominated Southern Rhodesia in a federation would greatly reduce the possibility of black rule, but, instead, the Federation speeded up the struggle for freedom. Up until this time, most Africans had believed that the British had their best interests in mind, despite the many instances of discrimination. Now they felt desperate.

Even during the prosperous years of the Federation, the Africans could see they were getting far less from the arrangement than the whites. For example, the federal government spent approximately $309 per European child for education, while in Northern Rhodesia only $27 per child was spent on African schooling. Africans worked in higher positions than they had held before, but they never advanced far enough to seriously threaten white power.

The African path to independence was not smooth. One complication was a division within the black leadership. Harry Nkumbula, originally considered a radical leader, became more and more moderate and willing to compromise with the Europeans. Kaunda and his closest friends, including Simon Kapwepwe, one of the more militant African leaders, were impatient with what they saw as something akin to a sellout on the part of Nkumbula. They resisted splitting with him for a long time because a united African front seemed so important in convincing the whites of their strength and seriousness. Finally, in 1958, Kaunda was elected president of a new African political party, the Zambia African National Congress (ZANC). For the first time the word "Zambia," coined by Kapwepwe from "Zambezia"—a name used by the earliest explorers—came into general use among both Africans and Europeans.

From this time on, the Africans and the federalists were on a direct collision course. The whites were determined to gain independence for the Federation as a whole. The Africans demanded the right to secede from the Federation and to gain independence with black majority rule for separate countries. "Freedom" and "One man—one vote" became the cries.

In 1957, Ghana had made history as the first black African country to gain independence. By 1960, Harold Macmillan, the British prime minister, was speaking of the "winds of change." Many African nations were becoming independent each year, so Zambians felt more confident in their demands than they would have felt acting alone.

The four years from 1959 to 1962 were a period of great tension. Each side acted and reacted more and more desperately.

Simon Kapwepwe (right), leader in the independence movement and later vice-president of Zambia. With him is the Litunga of the Lozi (second from right).

The whites looked at the violence and bloodshed of the Mau-Mau uprising that had just taken place in Kenya as part of the nationalist movement there and feared the same might occur in Northern Rhodesia. Many of their precautions may have been harsher than necessary because of this anxiety. The federal government declared a state of emergency along the line-of-rail in Northern Rhodesia following attempts by some African nationalists to derail trains as a show of strength.

In 1959, federal elections were scheduled, and ZANC urged that the Africans boycott them as a form of protest. As a result, the governor of Northern Rhodesia banned ZANC and called its leaders " 'racketeers' who had instituted a reign of terror, had practised witchcraft and threatened to kill or mutilate women and children." Fifty African leaders, including Kaunda and Kapwepwe, were arrested and sent to remote parts of the country. Months of protests and demonstrations followed. Several thousand Africans were imprisoned.

In June 1959, another African political party was formed to replace the forbidden ZANC. This new party was the one which was to bring Northern Rhodesia to independence. It was called the United National Independence Party (UNIP). At the end of his term of detention, Kaunda took over as its president.

The Africans' main show of strength was through organized boycotts of businesses owned by whites. Boycotts had been occurring since the early 1950s, but were now increased. Butchers and beer halls were frequent targets. Africans also made repeated attempts to gain service at restaurants or shops where they had been denied admittance. Laws to ban racial discrimination in Northern Rhodesia were passed in 1960, but the Africans found them too little, too late.

In 1961, the British saw the handwriting on the wall. Recognizing that they could no longer keep the Africans out of politics, they proposed a revised constitution that would allow Africans to vote in large numbers. Because this would enable Africans to achieve a majority in the legislature, Roy Welensky and others persuaded Great Britain to change the proposals. For the first time the Africans expressed their opposition in widespread violence. Their leaders were no longer in control. There was considerable property damage. Schools were burned. Roads were blocked. In one widely publicized incident, a white woman was attacked on the Copperbelt and killed, but there were few such cases of personal injury.

The British backed down and revised the constitution in the Africans' favor once again. In October 1962, the two African political parties (ANC and UNIP) joined together to form the first black government in Northern Rhodesia. Kenneth Kaunda was prime minister. The Federation dissolved with little notice at the end of 1963.

Independence for Zambia was now a foregone conclusion. Plans were made for the event to occur on October 24, 1964. The date was chosen both because it is United Nations Day and because it was the date of the founding of ZANC.

Kaunda faced three major problems as Independence Day approached. The Litunga of the Lozi insisted that Barotseland was a separate country. Fortunately for the unity of Zambia, a large number of the younger and politically active Lozi refused to support this view. At last, the Litunga reluctantly agreed to relinquish his claim and to allow Barotseland to join the nation of Zambia as an equal with other provinces.

Far to the north of Lusaka, another problem had been brewing for a number of years. In September 1953, Alice Lenshina, a former classmate of Kaunda, arrived at the Lubwa Mission, where they had both grown up, and announced that she had come back from the dead, not once, but four times. This rather plump and matronly-looking young woman of thirty-three used the visions she'd had during her "deaths" as the basis for a totally new African religion. Her followers became known as Lumpas.

The Lumpa religion was based on both Christianity and African tradition. It promised salvation for Africans, freedom from sorcery, and an escape from European domination. During the early years of the Federation, it enjoyed great success. In 1959, the Lumpa church had between fifty and one hundred thousand members.

But as the independence movement gained force, many Africans left the Lumpa religion and looked to political salvation instead. Lenshina saw the government, even a black government, as a threat to her authority. She forbade her followers to join a political party or to be involved with politics in any way. In some cases, Lumpas directly disobeyed orders of local government authorities. UNIP members punished them by burning Lumpa churches. Support for UNIP was very strong among the Bemba, and local members of UNIP regarded nonmembers as enemies of the nation.

Tension ran high. Kaunda met with Lenshina and tried to cool down the situation, but in the weeks just prior to Independence, war broke out between the Lumpas and the supporters of UNIP. Kaunda had to send in government forces, and in the end over seven hundred persons were killed. Lenshina and many of her followers were detained. She remained in exile until a Zambia High Court judge ordered her release in late 1973. It brought much grief to Kaunda that this should happen to the people in his own home district.

Finally, there was the question of mineral royalties still taken each year by the British South Africa Company. A long and dramatic series of negotiations carried out by representatives of the BSAC, Great Britain, and the African government of Northern Rhodesia ended just hours before Independence. Ten months before Independence the BSAC had been offered $150 million for the mineral rights to be paid back in equal payments through 1986 by the Zambian government. Emrys-Evans, the indecisive emissary for BSAC, could not make up his mind whether or not to accept. Meanwhile, a detailed study of the company was made for the Northern Rhodesian cabinet. The conclusion of this report was that the legal basis for the BSAC claims was very shaky. Backed up by this opinion, the Africans immediately took and maintained control of the situation. In the end, the BSAC had to agree to give up all mineral rights for a compensation of only $12 million. This was less than half the amount the BSAC received in royalties every year. The money which had been drained from Northern Rhodesia for many years would now be her own.

With these problems behind her and the future filled with brightness, midst garden parties and tribal dancing, Zambia became the thirty-sixth black African nation to achieve independence. For the citizens of the new nation, it seemed that night was over and dawn had come. Unfortunately, expectations of individuals for themselves and for their country were shattered only too soon. The struggle had really only just begun.

The constitution of the new Zambian nation called for a president to head the government. Kenneth Kaunda, the man who led Northern Rhodesia to independence and had served as her first prime minister, was elected to this office in the fall of 1964 and assumed his duties on Independence Day. It was Kaunda who now had to face the challenge of steering his country through the difficult times that lay ahead.

President Kaunda in the toga he wears on formal occasions.

9

A Humanist in Africa*

On April 27, 1967, President Kenneth Kaunda declared Humanism the national philosophy for the young nation of Zambia. Humanism is taught in every Zambian school, Grade 1 through the university level. No person is allowed to become a member of UNIP unless he is prepared to accept the principles of this Zambian doctrine. Workers are given time off from their jobs to discuss its meaning. A Ministry of National Guidance was created in 1969 to watch over the application of Humanism to all aspects of Zambian life. In late 1972, President Kaunda proclaimed a Humanism Week, during which both individuals and businesses concentrated on improving their practice of the nation's philosophy.

Humanism, as defined in Zambia, is based upon the way of life that was common in traditional Africa. Villagers worked together with the goal of providing the best for every individual. It was an unwritten law that help was always available to someone in need. Chiefs did not hoard vast supplies of food while common men went hungry. As applied to Zambia today, this means that the government must care for every one of the 4 million Zambian inhabitants; each person, in turn, must cooperate with and work for the good of his neighbor.

Zambia, like many other developing nations, has taken the position of nonalignment in world affairs, refusing to identify with either the Eastern or the Western power bloc. In following

* There is a book by this title. It is a collection of letters written by Kenneth Kaunda to his missionary friend, Colin Morris.

the doctrine of Humanism, Zambia has gone even further than some of her neighbors in rejecting both capitalism and communism. According to Zambian Humanism, capitalism seeks to take advantage of the common man while communism does not take account of the importance of the individual. The socialism practiced in many African nations is akin to Zambian Humanism but does not emphasize so strongly the responsibility of each man to every other.

This unique Zambian philosophy is grounded in high ideals, but so is the character of the man who has offered it to his country and to the world. Although he was only forty when he became the first president of Zambia in 1964, Dr. Kaunda has already had a great impact not only on his own nation but on much of the rest of the African continent as well.

Abraham Lincoln is an American whom President Kaunda greatly admires. The Zambian president has frequently referred to Lincoln's description of government "of the people, by the people, and for the people." Kaunda's interpretation of democratic rule for his people is one with which Lincoln might disagree, but at least the starting point of their thoughts on government was the same.

Parallels can be found in the lives of the two men. In 1924, at Lubwa in the northern part of Northern Rhodesia, Kenneth David Kaunda was born to missionary parents in a small dwelling that must have been similar to Lincoln's log cabin birthplace. Lincoln never forgot his simple origins. Neither has Kaunda, who always feels comfortable with the humblest of his people. In fact, until he became a government minister in 1962, Kaunda and his large family lived in a cramped two-room shack. And, like Lincoln, Kaunda grew up a rather reserved person who overcame his shyness to serve his country and his ideals.

Another trait of Lincoln's shared by Kaunda is a great thirst for knowledge. The death of his father when he was eight forced him to work extremely hard to earn his school fees. In 1939, Munali, the first government-run secondary school in Northern Rhodesia, was opened at Lusaka. Kenneth was overjoyed to be chosen the next year as one of twenty-nine entering pupils.

Here the young scholar was profoundly influenced by one of his teachers, Daniel Sonquishe, a man from the country of South Africa. In his autobiography, *Zambia Shall Be Free,* Kaunda relates a conversation with Sonquishe that he never forgot. Sonquishe told Kaunda about the ill-treatment of Africans by the white men in his country. "Kenneth," he said, "it is almost too late for us to do anything about it in South Africa; we've lost our chance, but here it is not too late. Young men like yourself must make sure that what happened to us in the south will never happen up here. It is up to you now."

Kaunda took these words to heart in fighting for the rights of his people. He made many personal protests against the discrimination suffered by Africans prior to Independence. For example, Kaunda swore never again to eat red meat because he refused to accept the humiliation of purchasing it at the butcher shops through a small window in the back. Even though this discrimination has long since ended, he has stuck by his promise and still eats no meat in order to remind himself and his countrymen of what the past was like and of the freedom they now enjoy.

Two years before he finished secondary school, Kaunda received an urgent plea from the missionaries at Lubwa to return immediately as a teacher. Kaunda has always been deeply committed to his religion and felt indebted to the mission where he grew up, so—as much as he wanted to stay at school—he responded to the call. Even with only two years of high school, Kaunda was one of the most educated Africans in the country.

After leaving school in 1941, Kaunda, in traditional African manner, married a girl chosen by his mother. His wife, Betty, and his children, who now number nine, have supported him throughout his political career, although often they would not see him for several months at a time.

A restlessness plagued Kaunda during his years of teaching. In 1947, he left Lubwa and journeyed briefly to Tanganyika and Southern Rhodesia in search of a more satisfying job. Conditions were so poor that after a few months he returned to Zambia and accepted a position as boarding master at a school in Mufulira on the Copperbelt. Betty joined him there and took a teaching job also.

Kaunda plunged enthusiastically into the activities of the Mufulira African Welfare Society. From this time on, he became more and more involved in politics. While on the Copperbelt, he was elected to the Urban Advisory Council and later the Provincial Council. In 1949, he and Betty decided to try their hands at farming and moved back to Lubwa. Here he and his friends organized a local branch of the African National Congress. As an enthusiastic officer of the ANC he traveled throughout the Northern Province by bicycle, organizing rallies and urging people to protest the injustices they were suffering.

Although lions roamed the countryside, Kaunda carried no weapon on his journeys, only a guitar. Music has always been a vital part of Kaunda's life. At the political meetings he led the people in singing hymns, folk songs, and a few selections he composed himself. He still brings his guitar to rallies, and playing it is one of his favorite relaxations at home.

From being a leader in the local ANC, Kaunda rapidly rose to national prominence. By 1955, Harry Nkumbula, the head of ANC, felt himself threatened by Kaunda's popularity. Eventually, the two Africans went their separate ways and Kaunda did emerge as the stronger.

During the independence struggle, Kaunda was imprisoned twice. In 1955, he was jailed for possessing "prohibited literature." The prohibited literature was a copy of the magazine *Africa and the Colonial World* with an article critical of the Northern Rhodesian government. In March 1959, all the leaders of the Zambia African National Congress were arrested for alleged illegal and disruptive political activities. Specifically, Kaunda was charged with calling an unauthorized meeting. Despite the treatment he received, Kaunda maintained his staunch belief in the doctrine of nonviolence, a belief that stemmed from his religious background and his admiration for the philosophy of India's leader, Mahatma Gandhi. Gandhi had brought nonviolence as a weapon for fighting oppression to the attention of the world. It has been used as a form of protest in many countries, including the United States.

In 1960, even as he emerged, weak and sick, from his dreary second prison term, Kaunda faced his people and proclaimed, "All I am asking the Africans of Northern Rhodesia is that they should remain calm and patient, and should prepare themselves for the real nonviolent struggle that lies ahead." Frequently he tied his urgings to an old Bemba saying: "There are more ways to kill a leopard than the use of a spear." Kaunda was in the forefront of the African leaders who insisted that their followers adhere to this lofty principle of passive resistance. It is largely to his credit that Zambia's road to independence was virtually free of the bloodshed and violence that occurred in countries such as the Congo, Kenya, and Algeria.

In order to promote Zambian national unity, Kaunda urges all his people to think of themselves as Zambians above all else. He encourages them to give their allegiance not to their own tribal groups but to the country as a whole. Although Kaunda grew up among the Bemba and speaks their language, he is not a member of any Zambian tribal group, as his parents belonged to a tribe in what is now the country of Malawi. In public speeches Kaunda always uses English rather than one of the tribal languages.

Unity is important to Kaunda not only within his own country but throughout the entire continent; he has long been a dedicated pan-Africanist. In 1971, he completed a term as head of the Organization of African Unity, which had been founded in 1963 to promote cooperation among the many African nations.

In many of the major conflicts that swept the African continent in the 1960s, Kaunda sought to bring peace. He risked his life in 1962 when he made a secret flight to the Katanga Province of the Congo in an attempt to reason with the secessionist leader, Moise Tshombe. His most notable success was overseeing the end to the long-term border disputes between Somalia, Ethiopia, and Kenya. When civil war swept Nigeria in the late 1960s, Zambia was one of four African nations to recognize the independence of the seceding region of Biafra. Kaunda had hoped that other nations would follow his lead. It was his belief that if Biafra had received sufficient support, the Nigerian federal government might have felt pressured to an early settlement, and peace could have been restored. In 1972, Kaunda was awarded the Nehru Peace Prize.

Because of his active leadership both at home and abroad, the handsome, kindly face of this tall and proud Zambian is familiar to most Africans. Kaunda is so well known, in fact, that the safari

President Kaunda in his characteristic outfit, a safari suit.

suits he frequently wears are advertised in East Africa as "Kaunda suits." Europeans and Africans alike affectionately refer to him by his initials, "K. K."

It would be well, perhaps, if we could stop our study of Kaunda here. Internationally, Kaunda continues to be thought of as the selfless man of stature described above. At home in his own country, some say Kaunda has changed and that the change has been for the worse.

Before Independence, Kaunda could afford to be an idealist; since Independence, he has been forced to become more of a practical politician. To those who have watched Kaunda closely since Independence, it seems that, on occasion, he has abandoned his ideals altogether. Once during the colonial days Kaunda commented on a group of men whom he had trusted and who he felt had betrayed him. Paraphrasing a statement made by the British philosopher, Lord Acton, Kaunda remarked, "They are in power, and power corrupts."

We would be judging Kaunda too harshly to say he has become corrupt, but being in power has made a difference. He has become more arbitrary, more authoritarian, and less humanistic in some of his actions than one might have predicted in 1964. Perhaps he has done as well as any human could, considering the great and varied challenges he has faced as the leader of independent Zambia. Or, perhaps, as a leader unable to find totally satisfactory solutions, he has turned more and more toward a simple effort to keep himself in control of the government as he and his country have faced complicated and urgent problems.

10

Problems of a New Nation

Zambia was one of the last colonies in Africa to become an independent nation. This put her in a position to learn from the mistakes of other new nations and to benefit from their successes. The wealth from her copper mines gave her the opportunity to use this knowledge and build a model country. For thirteen months this dream moved toward becoming a reality. But the happiness and optimism that followed freedom from colonial rule suddenly turned to anxiety and despair on November 11, 1965. On this day, Southern Rhodesia illegally declared herself independent from Great Britain.

Approximately 5 percent of the population of Southern Rhodesia is white, and this small minority holds almost absolute control over the 95 percent that is black. Britain had said that Southern Rhodesia could be independent only if the government had a plan for allowing the Africans to come into power. The white Rhodesians were not willing to give up their ruling position. If black rule ever does come, they said, it will be many, many years in the future. Therefore, without Britain's consent, Prime Minister Ian Smith proclaimed an independent "Republic of Rhodesia." This event is referred to as UDI for unilateral, or one-sided, declaration of independence.

Although UDI was not completely unexpected, it sent shock waves around the world. The independence of Southern Rhodesia was not recognized by any country. An emergency session of the United Nations Security Council was called. It was agreed that something should be done to stop the actions of the rebellious colony, but there was great disagreement on what should be done.

Naturally, Zambia was totally opposed to a country where a large black population was dominated by a small white population. President Kaunda offered Zambian territory as a base from which British troops could enter Rhodesia and put down the rebellion; this, he felt, was the only way to reverse what had happened. Britain had no intention of reacting this drastically to UDI, though it was several months before Kaunda understood this.

The British foreign secretary urged the United Nations Security Council to declare economic sanctions against Rhodesia rather than to advocate an invasion. After several days of debate, the Security Council honored Britain's request and passed a resolution asking all nations to stop any economic trade with Rhodesia, excluding medical and educational supplies. Under the United Nations Charter, this resolution should have been binding on all members. For a number of years most countries, at least officially, stated that they were totally boycotting trade with Rhodesia.

The leaders of Zambia had argued urgently that sanctions would not put an end to the illegal government, but no one listened. The difficulties with economic sanctions were many. Before the Rhodesian government declared UDI, it had anticipated what might happen. Knowing that economic punishment was highly possible, the government acted only when it felt the country was ready to withstand the hardships the boycotts would cause. Rhodesia also knew that a few countries, including her powerful neighbor to the south, South Africa, would ignore the sanctions and continue to give her some aid. Finally, economic sanctions depend on voluntary cooperation because they are almost impossible to enforce. As the years have gone by, some nations, including the United States, have resumed trade with Rhodesia despite their obligation not to.

The Organization of African Unity met in Addis Ababa on December 3, 1965, and declared that all members should break diplomatic relations with Great Britain unless she used force against Rhodesia. Some countries followed this edict, at great cost, but many others did not. Several African countries offered to send troops, but Kaunda maintained that this was the duty of Great Britain.

Zambia joined other countries in trying to break off economic relations with Rhodesia. The economy of no other country, not even that of Rhodesia, was affected as severely as that of Zambia. The problem for landlocked Zambia was that the vast majority of both her imports and exports at the time of UDI either came from Rhodesia or traveled on the rail line through Rhodesia. Ninety-five percent of all imports came this way, and all copper was exported on the Rhodesian rail. The attempt to cut off commerce through and from Rhodesia resulted in shortages of many essential materials, and great expense was incurred in obtaining supplies by more difficult routes. Money that would have been spent on education, medical services, and general improvement of life in Zambia had to be used to meet the emergencies caused by UDI.

Britain, Canada, and the United States came to Zambia's aid with emergency airlifts of petrol (gasoline) and other fundamental products that were no longer available from Rhodesia. It was estimated that in the first three years after UDI, Zambia spent $112 million on fuel transport alone. At times Zambians were allowed as little as one gallon of petrol per week.

Not only did Zambia suffer severe shortages of essentials such as fuel oil and coal, but the supply of electrical power was threatened. The power station was located on the Rhodesian side of Kariba, so the Rhodesian government controlled the distribution of electrical power. A cutoff would have caused flooding of the copper mines as well as other disasters.

President Kaunda demanded that Great Britain compensate Zambia for her enormous financial losses because Britain's refusal to use force had caused them. Britain responded with some monetary aid, but nothing close to what Zambia needed.

If Zambia planned to decrease her dependence on Rhodesian facilities, it was obvious that her own would have to be improved. It became only too clear how Zambian money had been used

Kariba Dam.

during the period of the Federation to build up Southern Rhodesia, leaving Zambia with very little to call her own.

The first project to aid the Zambians was a 1,060-mile pipeline to bring in petrol from Dar es Salaam in Tanzania, the nearest friendly seaport. The pipeline was built by the Italians and opened in the summer of 1968, almost three years after UDI. An oil refinery has been built at Ndola on the Copperbelt and a second pipeline is under construction by the same Italian firm. Before the pipeline was completed, the only alternative Zambia had to bringing oil through Rhodesia or via short-term airlifts was truck transport along the Great North Road from Dar es Salaam. The rough, untarred road, inches deep in dust and filled with ruts in the dry season, and feet deep in red mud during the rainy season, well deserved its nickname, "Hell Run." The drivers who made the route were well paid, but many lost their lives, and the road was littered with trucks, wrecked and abandoned.

Despite the hardships, Zambia's efforts to decrease her dependence on Rhodesian goods and transportation routes paid off. Zambia reduced her imports of Rhodesian goods from 60 percent of total imports in 1964 to 7 percent in 1969. These figures do not include, however, items merely transported through Rhodesia. At the same time, Zambia drastically reduced her exports through Rhodesia. Her exports through Dar grew from 39,000

Construction of pipeline to Dar es Salaam.

tons of goods in 1966 to 231,000 tons in 1969. Even so, Zambia had to continue to send half her copper through Rhodesia and to receive two-thirds of her goods this way.

The other ambitious project undertaken by Zambia was the Tan-Zam or Tazara railway, a joint venture with Tanzania. Plans for this had been initiated even before UDI, but UDI made critical the building of the railway as an alternative transport route. President Kaunda sought financial help from England, the United States, the World Bank, and the United Nations, but all felt that the rail would take too long to build and would not pay its way. Then, to everyone's surprise, the People's Republic of China came through with an offer of an interest-free $406 million loan to be paid back over thirty years beginning in 1983, as compared with the 7 percent loan for construction of the second pipeline to be repaid to Italy over twelve years. The 1,163-mile railroad links the Zambian Copperbelt with the port at Dar. It was the largest overseas aid project Peking had ever undertaken and the longest railway the Chinese had ever built. An agreement was signed in September 1967. Actual construction began in 1970 and was to be completed by the end of 1976. The Chinese were consistently ahead of schedule and expected to finish the railroad almost two years early.

The Great Uhuru (freedom) Railway, as it is known, opens large portions of both Tanzania and Zambia for agricultural development as well as for possible mining and industrial development. In addition, over thirty-seven thousand Africans, about one-third of them Zambians, have been employed; this has created a large work force in both countries with construction skills. Zambians and Tanzanians are being trained in Dar and Peking to eventually take over complete management of the railway.

Between fifteen and twenty thousand Chinese arrived to work on the railroad, eight thousand of these in Zambia. These Chinese have generally kept both their thoughts and those of Chairman Mao to themselves. Few know English, or any African language, so there is little communication between the African and the Chinese workers. Only a few hundred Chinese were to remain once the job was completed, although Zambia has entered into other aid agreements with China. In February 1974, President Kaunda made an eight-day official visit to China. He had many words of praise for the Chinese people and their leaders.

Zambia agreed to import over $10 million per year of Chinese goods to help pay wages and other local costs not covered in the loan. One problem arising from this has been the competition of Chinese products with those produced by new local industries. For example, the sale of cloth manufactured in Zambia has suffered.

UDI also hastened Zambia's efforts to generate her own electrical power. In 1971, the first stage of the Kafue hydroelectric scheme, just south of Lusaka, was completed, and it was in full production in 1972. It was constructed by Yugoslavia's Energoprojekt. Work is under way on a Kariba North Bank power station. Great Britain has agreed to repay for Zambia a loan of around $260,000 which is helping to finance this underground power station. With these projects, Rhodesia has lost one of her principal threats against Zambia.

Zambia's copper mines depend on coal, most of which Zambia imported from Rhodesia at the rate of about 110,000 tons per month before UDI. Zambia immediately set to work developing her own coal deposits. In 1966, a coal field near Lake Kariba was put into production, but it was later closed when enough coal of higher quality was obtained from a new mine at Maamba in the Southern Province. Zambia no longer needs Rhodesian coal.

Some argue that UDI was a blessing for Zambia in that it forced her to push forward with development projects and means to becoming more independent years before she would have otherwise. There is no doubt, however, that the Zambian people have been called upon to endure the hardships of higher prices, drastic shortages, and a sad slowdown in the development of social services.

UDI has probably been Zambia's biggest problem since Independence, but certainly not her only one. During the 1960s and early 1970s, in the Portuguese colonies of Mozambique and Angola, to the east and west of Zambia, small wars were going on. Freedom fighters (or terrorists, depending on which side of the conflict one supports) were attempting to win the countries for African rule.

Portuguese soldiers attempted to suppress the Africans and carried out hostile acts against Zambians because they knew the Zambian government and people were in sympathy with the Africans seeking liberation. Zambian villagers and police officers close to the boundaries were killed, wounded, or kidnapped. In August 1972, the Zambian government ordered all Zambian villages bordering Angola and Mozambique to be evacuated because of increasing attacks by Portuguese soldiers.

Zambia did lend support to the freedom fighters when possible. The Zambian government allowed FRELIMO, the freedom fighters' organization in Mozambique, to set up a radio station in Lusaka from which they could broadcast into Mozambique one hour each day.

Zambia, nonetheless, had to depend on shipping a number of imports and exports through Portuguese territories, and so maintained a sort of peace. The Portuguese often retaliated against the Zambians in subtle ways. For example, in 1971, an enormous shipment of wheat was delayed in Mozambique for months. The Portuguese denied that they were holding up the goods due for Zambia and blamed "technical difficulties." At one point a high tariff was placed on Zambian copper exported through ports in Angola.

In 1974, a drastic change occurred in Portuguese-African relations. Up until this time the Portuguese government had maintained that Mozambique and Angola were provinces of the mother country and there was no chance for independence. Then, on April 25, the military overthrew the government in Portugal and immediately announced that they were willing to consider independence for the Portuguese colonies in Africa. For the first time the leaders of the freedom fighters sat to talk with government officials. Firm steps toward independence were taken with the proposal of a referendum to be held in Angola during March 1975. In Mozambique a provisional government was set up in September 1974 with plans for a complete African takeover on June 25, 1975.

The new Portuguese policy may have far-reaching effects on the balance of power in all of southern Africa. In governing her colonies, Portugal has always sided with Rhodesia and South Africa in official policies. A black-controlled government in these territories probably would not. A short-term benefit for Zambia will be that she can ship exports through these territories without pangs of conscience or fear of sabotage. Already in 1974, over half of her $800 million worth of copper ore exports traveled along the Benguela Railroad to the port of Lobito in Angola.

With the railroad through Dar es Salaam finished and increased opportunity for transport through Mozambique and Angola, Zambia may at last be freed from dependence on any one route to the sea. Despite the convenience of the railway through Tanzania, Zambia may have to rely more and more on alternative routes because of the high cost of handling charges in East Africa. In 1974, the East Africa Harbour Corporation announced a 400 percent increase in these assessments. In addition, the harbor at Dar is becoming more and more overcrowded.

Zambia's other neighbor to the east, Malawi, has a black African government, but at times relations between Zambia and Malawi have been strained because of Malawi's policy toward South Africa. Malawi is one of the few African countries that support dialogue and trade with South Africa. Zambia still gets a great many of her imports from South Africa, especially heavy equipment vital to the mines, but does so only through necessity and with the belief that someday she will no longer have to.

Zambia has had many internal problems also. Immediately following Independence, racial tensions were high and this problem is still not completely resolved. UDI, with its focus on black-white tensions, did not help any. There is also friction within the black population. President Kaunda has tried to distribute high government positions among the various tribes, but members of one tribe or another almost always feel (and sometimes actually are) discriminated against. The efforts at balance have, at times, caused more problems than they have solved.

When Zambia gained independence, there were two major political parties. Since then, several others have been formed, but none lasted for long. Most of them were banned by President Kaunda on the basis that they were disrupting peaceful government. The most significant political event of Zambia's history was the declaration in 1972 of a one-party state. This means that all political parties except UNIP are illegal.

Although the banning of all but one political party would be an unacceptable act in the United States, it is not an unnatural act for a country facing the many internal and external uncertainties that confront Zambia. It is wise to look at this step in the context of African governments in general. In 1972, only three other African countries out of approximately fifty had more than one political party. All other independent black African states were either one-party states, monarchies, or military governments. So Zambia, under the guidance of Kaunda, followed a course not at all unusual for a developing nation.

Zambia legally became a one-party state by an act of Parliament on December 13, 1972. During the preceding year, a commission set up by President Kaunda traveled around Zambia seeking people's suggestions for the form the government should take. The commission was headed by the vice-president, Mainza Chona. The members of the commission submitted a lengthy report to the president based on statements made at public hearings. After reviewing the suggestions made by the people, President Kaunda and his advisors wrote a new constitution to replace the one written at the time of Independence. This new document was presented to the Zambian Parliament in the summer of 1973. Elections for a new parliament and for president were scheduled for the fall of 1973.

Under Zambia's second constitution there is a president with full executive powers. He must be at least thirty-five and can serve an unlimited number of five-year terms. There is also a prime minister appointed by the president from members of

Parliament to serve as the president's spokesman. The president also appoints a secretary-general to run UNIP. The secretary-general is second in the government power structure. The prime minister must follow his directives. The Parliament, or National Assembly, as it is more commonly called, consists of 136 members: 125 elected, 10 appointed by the president, and a Speaker elected by the members. The constitution also provides for a 27-member House of Chiefs. The chiefs can submit legislation to the president, who decides whether or not to bring it before the National Assembly, so they have no real power. Only UNIP members can run for political posts.

The first elections under the new constitution were held on December 5, 1973. President Kaunda received over 80 percent of the vote and on December 10 was sworn in for his third five-year term as president of Zambia.

To outside observers and to some Zambians, the most disturbing part of Zambian politics is not the form the government takes nor the absence of more than one political party, but the

National Assembly Building.

oppression by those in power of those who are not. For many years now, the slogan of the ruling party has been, "It pays to belong to UNIP." This slogan was to be taken seriously in a very real and practical sense. Although officially UNIP membership is voluntary, not only are those who belong to UNIP rewarded, but those who do not are punished. A particularly unruly branch of the party is the "UNIP Youths." Before Zambia became a one-party state, these youths would go from house to house or set up roadblocks and demand to see each person's UNIP membership card. Frequently a person could not enter a store or ride a bus without a UNIP card. Sometimes those found without such a card were physically attacked.

In August 1971, Simon Kapwepwe, former vice-president and the minister of provincial and local government and culture, resigned to form his own political party, known as the United People's Party. In February 1972, this party was declared illegal, and 123 of its members were arrested and kept in prison almost a year. Twice in the month preceding, Kapwepwe was assaulted on the streets of Lusaka by UNIP members, severely beaten, and stripped of his clothes. Although President Kaunda condemned this attack, there have been times when his remarks have incited crowds to just such actions, and he has acted as if anyone not supporting UNIP and/or his own personal programs is a traitor to the country. In short, the president has not always strongly exerted his leadership to stop needless cruelty and violence.

Slowly and rather quietly, President Kaunda has gathered more and more power into his own hands. He can detain anyone in prison for any length of time without trial if that person is declared a threat to national security. The president has also been authorized to spend money without seeking the approval of the National Assembly.

How strong is President Kaunda's position as head of the government? Military coups d'etat are not uncommon on the African continent. Following the January 1971 coup in Uganda, a country not far to the north of Zambia, security measures in Zambia were tightened. For a time, troops were stationed at the airport and other strategic locations. In January 1973, the Zambia defense minister, Mr. Gray Zulu (later to be appointed secretary-general of UNIP), announced that there had been an unsuccessful attempt to organize a military coup against the government. In May 1973, nine top military officials, including three colonels, were removed from office. In some African countries a change to a one-party state has been followed rather quickly by a military coup. Attempts are being made to actively include Zambian military personnel in the government, with the hopes of maintaining their loyalty. Harry Nkumbula, Kaunda's chief rival since preindependence days, joined UNIP in the summer of 1973, so there is at least a surface unity in the country. So far, the Zambian government has been remarkably stable. Only time will tell if it will remain so.

Zambia had just begun to settle the question of what form the new government would take when yet another crisis with Rhodesia arose. On January 9, 1973, Rhodesia declared her borders with Zambia completely closed. This meant an end to all imports and exports along the rail line through Rhodesia to the port of Beira in Mozambique. Zambia, of course, had attempted to lessen the traffic along this route for the past seven years, but she still depended on the Rhodesia route for around half of her copper exports and for over fifty thousand tons of imports per month. Rhodesia immediately announced that she would make an exception for Zambia's copper exports; in fact, this was not just kindness on the part of Rhodesia, but arose from her need for the $25 million per year the railroad earned from transit taxes.

To understand why Rhodesia took the drastic action of closing her borders, it is necessary to look at what had been happening within the country in the few months previous to the decision. It had become apparent that Rhodesia would not compromise, so force seemed the only way for Africans to obtain any political power there. Rhodesia, like the Portuguese territories, became a target for attacks by freedom fighters.

The Rhodesian rebels stepped up their attacks in parts of Rhodesia close to the Zambian border. The incident which immediately preceded the border closure was a land mine explosion on a track near the Zambezi River. Two Rhodesian policemen were wounded and two South African policemen who had been sent to aid the Rhodesians were killed. Headquarters of one of the Rhodesian black African political parties in Lusaka claimed credit for this and three other incidents since August 1972. Ian Smith, head of the Rhodesian government, acted in a state of panic. His reason for closing the border was to force Zambia to be tougher on the rebels and to stop them from training on and launching attacks from Zambian soil.

It was Zambia's turn to make the next move after Rhodesia's announcement. On January 11, to the surprise of many, including the Rhodesian government, Zambia announced that she would not accept the exception made by Rhodesia, that no more copper exports or any other exports would go through Rhodesia, and that she would consider the border permanently sealed.

When Rhodesia declared her UDI, the act was extremely unpopular with most countries, but the move was widely supported within Rhodesia and by her Portuguese and South African allies. Not so with the border closure of 1973. Within Rhodesia, the ruling whites were angered either because Smith did not go far enough, or because he had brought an even greater hardship on the population with the loss of Zambian revenue and seemed to gain little except an opportunity to look very foolish. Ian Smith himself said, "History may prove it was the wrong decision." One of South Africa's newspapers editorialized that, "Mr. Smith should realize that the obligation to his friends down south is to find solutions to existing problems, not to create new ones." Even Portugal came to the aid of Zambia rather than praising Rhodesia.

Rhodesia apparently still did not believe that Zambia would seriously cut off all trade. On February 4, Smith made a statement that he had been reassured by the government in Lusaka that the "terrorists were not operating from Zambian soil." Based upon this communication, he pronounced the border open once more. Zambia replied swiftly and firmly: the border was to remain closed. The giant butterfly, Zambia, was now irrevocably headed away from her overdependence on hostile governments to the south. Complete cutting of all ties with Rhodesia was something some Zambians had advocated as far back as UDI, but at that time there simply were not enough alternative routes available. In 1973, the time was still not as ripe as Zambia would have desired, but survival under the loss was possible.

President Kaunda made it very clear that Zambia's dedication to her principles and her example to the rest of the world would mean even more sacrifice in material goods and comforts than Zambian citizens had known in the past. Special agencies were set up to determine import quotas. Mining supplies and medical equipment received top priority. Industrial supplies came next. Consumer goods ranked lowest. Once again Zambians prepared to tighten their belts.

As had happened after UDI, many nations offered help to Zambia. Canada was the first, with $8 million to build up alternative transportation routes. China supplied more than two-thirds of the immediate cash grants. Norway provided the second largest gift. A four-country team was sent by the United Nations Security Council to study the situation in Zambia. As a result of this study, the Security Council passed a resolution on March 10, 1973, directing Dr. Waldheim "to organise immediately financial, technical and material assistance to Zambia to enable it to face the challenge arising from the economic blockade imposed by Smith."

Routes through Tanzania, Kenya, Angola, and Mozambique (via Malawi rather than Rhodesia) were worked out. The Tan-Zam Railway stood only a year from completion at the time of border closure. The Tanzanian section was already in operation and could be used to transport items brought to the end of the line by truck. Zambia sought and received help in assembling a fleet of one thousand extra trucks to help with road transport. Kenya added over one hundred trucks to her own fleet to carry imports and exports. Germans with Lufthansa Airlines and the French with UTA airlifted important supplies to Zambia, including those from South Africa. Tanzania offered the port at Dar es Salaam for Zambian imports and exports alone, diverting her own supplies to a harbor farther north.

At least temporarily, Zambia has found a solution to most of her problems. One which persists, however, is fear of attack by South Africa. South Africans accuse Zambia of allowing training for guerrilla warfare to occur on Zambian soil. President Kaunda has denied these accusations, but the South Africans continue to harass Zambia whenever possible. There have been repeated incidents in which Zambian civilians, policemen, and members of the armed forces have been severely wounded or killed by land mines. Zambia places the blame for these incidents on South Africans, who, she says, cross into Zambia through the Caprivi Strip, a small section of South-West Africa which borders Zambia. With the help of Great Britain, Zambia has tried to arm herself against a possible air attack, but she can never feel completely secure.

The events of the past ten years make it seem that Zambia has nothing but troubles. There is, however, a part of her life which is bright and strong—copper.

11

Where Copper Is King

Copper is the economic cornerstone of Zambian life. Absolutely every Zambian is affected in some way, either directly or indirectly, by what happens in the copper mines. During the years since Independence, copper and its most important by-product, cobalt, have accounted for somewhere between 93 and 97 percent of Zambia's exports. Year after year, the government has received approximately 60 percent of its revenue directly from copper. If copper prices are high, the economy of Zambia booms; if they are low, it sags.

In a sense, the world, as well as Zambia herself, depends on Zambian copper. Russia and the United States are the only countries which produce more copper than Zambia. Zambia exports more of her refined copper than either of these other two leading producers. In 1973, over 700,000 tons of copper were extracted from the eight mines then open on the Zambian Copperbelt and were sent to more than thirty countries around the world. Even the United States purchases Zambian copper.

Two qualities of copper make it almost invaluable: it lasts practically forever because of its resistance to corrosion, and it is particularly suitable for conducting both heat and electricity. Copper by itself is easy to work with, to mold into many different forms. Copper mixed with other metals can become tough and resistant. Bronze is an alloy of copper plus tin from which weapons and other objects requiring strength have long been made. Brass is copper plus zinc. Besides copper in its pure form and copper alloys, of which there are more than three thousand, there are many by-products of the copper-mining process with commercial and strategic value. Sulfuric acid is an example. Copper plus various acids forms copper salts such as copper chloride, which is used to purify swimming water. Copper has frequently been used in artistic and decorative works, also. Standing in New York Harbor is America's most famous piece of copper, the Statue of Liberty.

But can copper be replaced or overproduced, either of which would spell disaster for Zambia? In some instances, aluminum and plastic have taken over a few of copper's former tasks, but in general, nothing has been discovered with the needed properties of copper. Aluminum has only 60 percent of copper's conductivity. The demand for copper is steadily growing. Not only are more and more countries increasing the use of electrical and telephone wire, but the inventions of modern science, such as the computer and the space ship, depend heavily upon copper. Predictions are that the world's need for copper will more than triple in the next thirty years.

No one is sure exactly how long ago copper was found in the parts of Africa south of the Sahara Desert. Perhaps the Bantu peoples brought the knowledge of this exciting metal with them as they gradually migrated southward. By the time the early Portuguese explorers arrived in Central Africa, the Africans had not only discovered copper, but had mined it, smelted it (smelting is the extracting of the pure copper from the rock in which it is most frequently found; extreme heat is used to melt the copper into a liquid state), and molded it into various shapes and forms.

Copper may have been mined in Zambia for as long as two thousand years. The peoples of Zambia used copper as an ornament or as a type of currency, rather than for creating weapons. Bodies found at the archaeological site of Ingombe Ilede had their arms and legs wrapped in copper bangles. The Bemba man presented his betrothed a gift of a copper bracelet in somewhat the same manner that engagement rings are given today. When copper was money, it was frequently cast in the shape of a large X. The heavier it was, the more it could purchase. Copper coils also had a value as currency.

A Kaonde coppersmith, smelting copper in the traditional manner.

Much ceremony surrounded the process of mining and smelting. Prayers were offered to the spirits, and the rituals had the aura of a religious occasion. People associated with the mining operations held positions of prestige in the society. Usually, only one clan knew the secrets of the trade. The person most revered was the master smelter; his work was a closely guarded mystery and was controlled by many taboos. Mining was an integral part of traditional Zambian life until it was disrupted by the slave trading and resulting tribal warfare.

The procedures worked out by the early Zambians almost exactly parallel those used in twentieth-century mining operations. Present-day techniques are more sophisticated but follow the same basic steps. A great deal of skill and ingenuity was required to map out the complicated methods of separating the copper from the stone and then purifying it.

But how was copper ever found in the first place? What did it look like? Pure copper, with reddish gold tones, does exist in nature and, no doubt, this was the original type to be discovered. But most copper was spewed forth in a liquid form from the center of the earth some 600 million years ago and was forced into the pores of rocks, where it hardened. Probably a stone containing copper dropped into a fire by accident gave man the first clues to extracting copper from its ore. Once man realized that stones containing copper did exist, their presence was often easy to detect. One of the most common copper ores, for example, is malachite, which has a sparkling green color.

A story told to anyone inquiring into the history of Zambia's copper mines has to do with malachite. In 1902, a prospector named William Collier was out hunting one day when he chanced upon and shot a roan antelope. Near where the curved horns of the antelope fell, Collier noted a vivid green rock, a rock containing copper. The mine that was developed on this spot much later was given the name Roan Antelope; it is located at the Copperbelt town of Luanshya.

Numerous European prospectors, similar to the tough fortune hunters of the American West, combed the Copperbelt during the early years of this century. Their best clues were traces of mines worked much earlier by the Africans. By 1910, most of the large mineral deposits had been located and claims had been staked. None, however, were considered worth developing at the time. Mines in the United States alone were producing enough copper to supply the world's demand. At this time, also, the copper just to the north of Zambia in the Katanga Province of the Congo was considered much superior to that found in Zambia. The money it would take to expand mining in Zambia was not available.

The turning point for copper mining in Zambia was to come ten years later. Copper ores are divided into two categories, oxide and sulfide. Oxide ores lie near the surface, and it is more difficult to extract the copper from them than from sulfide ores, which are found deeper in the earth. The Zambia oxide ores contain a relatively small amount of copper. It was not until the 1920s that extensive drilling revealed the rich deposits of sulfide ores far below the surface. At the same time the demand for copper increased with the need for more and more electrical wire. Money began to pour into the area from investors in England, the United States, and South Africa.

The mosquito-infested Zambian Copperbelt, an area approximately thirty by ninety miles, was, at this time, covered by swamps and was one of the least healthy places in Africa. It was not a very appealing place to live. Europeans, therefore, had to be attracted by extremely high wages and other luxuries, a situation that was to cause many problems for Zambia in later years. A network of roads was spread over the land, towns boomed, and immigrants both from outside the country and from within flooded the area. When disaster, in the form of the depression, struck the world in the early 1930s, the Zambian Copperbelt suffered as well, but only a decade later it enjoyed an enormous boom with the increased need for copper during World War II. It was in the 1940s, in fact, that Zambia took her lead among the copper-producing countries of the world.

Copper mines are of two types: open pit and underground. Both kinds exist in Zambia, although three-quarters of the copper from Zambian mines comes from underground. This is in contrast to the United States, where the majority of the copper mines are open pit, or above ground. Underground mining is more expensive and more dangerous, but it makes sense when the ore deposits are at a great depth, as many in Zambia are. Underground mines are favored by ecologists, as open pit mines leave jagged scars on the face of the earth.

A closer look at a Zambian mine, both above and underground, and at the smelting process by which the copper is taken from the ore, will bring into focus the mammoth nature of the whole mining process on this remote central African plateau. The Rokana Division of the Nchanga Consolidated Copper Mines is located in the township of Nkana, the mine city adjacent to Kitwe. Three shafts plunge deep into the earth, opening the way for men and machinery. The Mindola shaft is the one described below.

Miners' clothing is required for all who go underground. A hard hat, a flashlight which can be attached to it, and heavy boots are protection against dangers that lie in wait. Falling rock, darkness, and flooding water can, alone or together, spell disaster. Fortunately, safety is now considered the right of each miner and much effort has been spent in keeping hazards to a mini-

A crosscut drive or main underground tunnel.

mum. Despite all precautions, tragedies can occur. The worst in
Zambian mining history was on September 25, 1970, at the Mufulira Mine, one of the largest underground mines in the world.
A massive cave-in, which filled tunnels with torrents of rushing
mud, water, and debris, killed eighty-nine men. After donning
protective clothing, the miners step aboard a skip, or large, open
elevator, which speeds underground.

As they go about their work, the miners speak to one another
in a totally unique language, Chikabanga. It is spoken nowhere
in the world other than in the mines of southern Africa. Because
the laborers were originally recruited not only from many parts
of Zambia but from the mines of South Africa as well, communication was very difficult. The problem solved itself with the
development of this unique language, partly English, partly
French, partly numerous Bantu tongues, smattered with Ger-
man and Afrikaans.

Crosscut drives, or tunnels, branch out from the elevator shaft
every 250 feet. In a cave, just below the earth's surface, the air is
often cool. However, in a mine, which goes far, far deeper, the
air gets warmer and warmer as it approaches the gases at the
center of the earth. At the last level of the Mindola Mine, almost
four thousand feet down, the air temperature is 114 degrees
Fahrenheit, and air conditioning is necessary. Even at the 2,880-
foot level, where temperatures are more comfortable, rapid cir-
culation of air is required.

A train with open cars is waiting to whisk the workers through
a light and airy tunnel complete with gleaming whitewashed
walls and sparkling lights overhead. Although most of the actual
mining work is done in much smaller, dimly lit tunnels that run
parallel to this large one, being greeted by space and light makes
the underground seem less awesome.

Tiny droplets of moisture glisten on the walls and little
streams run along the side of the tracks. More than 9 million
gallons of water are pumped out of this mine each day. Mindola
is not an extremely wet mine; from the Bancroft Mine, known as
the wettest mine in the world, over 65 million gallons are
pumped daily. At Mindola this water is cooled and recirculated

in the air-cooling and refrigeration systems, so a potential disaster is turned into an asset.

Leaving the main tunnel, from now on proceeding by foot, the workers enter a smaller tunnel, known as a hanging-wall drive, where men are drilling in preparation for blasting. The copper here is embedded in solid walls of rock. The holes in which the explosives are inserted must be carefully placed, in exact size, shapes, and patterns. Often the explosives are inserted as long as two months before the actual blast occurs. Premature explosion is a constant danger, but one which seldom materializes. The farther down in the mine, the more pressure is exerted on the charges by the increasing tonnage of earth and equipment above. An American explosive corporation has worked for some time on developing powder which resists this tension more successfully than any previously known; it has been evolved as a by-product of the space program's rocket fuel.

Blasting occurs daily. The ore loosened by the explosion is loaded onto a train. One of the most taxing underground jobs is the nightly cleaning of the tunnels where blasting has taken place; this is done by workers called "the lashing crew."

Before the ore is taken above ground, it goes into a giant crusher where, with much grinding, smashing, and beating, the rocks are broken into pieces no larger than six inches in diameter. The ore is now ready to leave the mine. In an average month, over 250,000 tons of ore are taken from the Mindola shaft of this mine, but only approximately 1.8 percent of the rock is copper. Obviously, much work is involved between the mining of the ore and the finished product.

The miner's surroundings are different at the Nchanga Mine, an open pit mine north of Kitwe near the town of Chingola. Nchanga is one of the largest open pit mines in the world, over a mile deep and three hundred feet across. Blasting and crushing are part of open pit mining as well, but the approach to the copper ore differs dramatically in the above ground mine. The open pit mine resembles a giant spiral with a huge coil at the top, going around and around downward, with each circle a tiny bit

An open pit mine on the Zambian Copperbelt.

smaller. Enormous "steps" are blasted out of the rock, and roads wind their way down to the bottom of the pit.

Trucks carry from one to two hundred tons of ore at a time and serve as a huge conveyor belt in and out of the mine. The tires on one of these trucks are taller than a full-grown woman or man. Driving these vehicles is a task requiring both skill and emotional stability. Steam shovels with buckets carrying twenty-five tons at a bite lift the blasted ore into the waiting trucks. This time the crusher is at the top of the mine.

Back at the Rokana Mine is the largest smelter in the world. It serves several mines throughout the Copperbelt, including the ones at Nchanga.

When the ore reaches the smelter, it has already gone through the concentrator. There it was crushed to the consistency of face powder and processed so that the copper level has now risen to 30 to 40 percent of the ore. This copper was separated from part of the waste, or gangue, by a process of flotation, or "catching" the copper particles. Legend has it that a miner's wife in the United States first suggested the principles involved when she observed tiny metal particles adhering to the soap bubbles while washing her husband's mining overalls.

When it arrives at the smelter, the copper ore is melted by intense heat in long, flat furnaces. The heavier metals, principally copper and iron, are ladled off the bottom of the furnaces as part of a substance called matte. The matte is poured into another type of furnace where compressed air is blown through the fiery hot copper. Valuable by-products are captured during this part of the purification, particularly sulfur for sulfuric acid. The copper is now 99 percent pure. It is known as blister copper because when it hardens, tiny blisters, representing the 1 percent of impurities, lie on the surface. This copper can be used, but is not pure enough yet for excellent conductivity.

Even purer copper is obtained by "poling"—the use of logs, from trees grown on the Copperbelt, to draw off more impurities—and then electrolytic refining. In the latter process the copper is dissolved in a solution of sulfuric acid through which an electric current is run. After it is refined to the purest state possible, copper is poured into molds, usually in a bar shape, to harden for shipping. The copper is now ready to make its way into the marketplaces of the world.

And what about the mine worker as a person? Frequently, he has been uprooted from his village and placed in a society of rapid change. He has a chance to earn money and provide better food, clothing, housing, and schooling for a family, but he also has to face a whole new set of problems. What has been said about urban problems in general applies very specifically to the worker recruited from village life to the mines. There are now, of course, some workers who were born and raised in a city environment and, for them, the adjustment is not so difficult.

The mines have always provided their employees with some sort of housing, education, recreation, and health facilities. But, until recently, although adequate, these facilities were so far below those available to the Europeans that they served frequently as a reminder of the implied inferiority of an African worker.

For many, many years, Africans were allowed to fill only the

Miners drilling in preparation for blasting.

lowest positions in the mines. Now "Zambianization," the replacement of non-Zambians by Zambians, is stressed at every level of mine work. In 1972, of the approximately three thousand underground workers at the Mindola shaft of the Rokana Mine only thirty-nine were Europeans, in contrast to a time when non-Zambians monopolized all but the most menial tasks. At this time, all of the very top-level management positions are still held by Europeans. This situation will be corrected as soon as there are qualified Zambians to fill the positions. The difference between today and yesterday is that now Zambians are actually at universities and on the job being trained to meet the qualifications.

The two major mining companies are Nchanga Consolidated Copper Mines, formerly the Anglo-American Corporation, and Roan Consolidated Mines, formerly the Roan Selection Trust. Smaller mining concerns account for less than 1 percent of investments on the Copperbelt. The largest stockholder in the Roan Consolidated Mines, after the Zambian government, is a United States firm, American Metal Climax, Inc.

Thirteen percent of the world's reserves of copper lie on the Zambian Copperbelt. Moreover, there are now several copper mines operating in parts of Zambia removed from the Copperbelt. Millions of dollars continue to be spent on prospecting, using advanced scientific detection methods, so perhaps even more mineral deposits will be found. Zambian copper, then, will continue to be important to people everywhere, and most of all to the Zambians themselves.

That the copper industry cannot survive alone hardly needs to be said. Not only are other industries necessary to support the copper mines, but other industries are critical to protect Zambia when copper prices fall. The country has always been much too dependent on one commodity. Attempts are now under way to give Zambia greater economic security.

12

A Borrowed Fiddle...

Proverbs or folk sayings are often the best way to express the truth of a situation. An old proverb of the Rhodesians says, "A borrowed fiddle does not finish a tune." One of Zambia's greatest problems since Independence is that so very much upon which she depends—talent, money, and goods—has been borrowed from other countries. The leaders of Zambia have realized that the country cannot be fully independent while she is so deeply in debt to others. The story of the Zambian economy in the past few years tells of a second battle for independence.

The most significant day in Zambia's economic history was April 19, 1968. On this day President Kaunda announced that in the future non-Zambian citizens would find it difficult to obtain credit at banks and that non-Zambians would not be able to operate businesses outside the ten major cities. (Later reforms went even further by preventing non-Zambians from owning *any* retail or wholesale business except for twenty specific categories after January 1, 1972.) These new rules became known as the "Mulungushi Reforms" after the place, a conference center north of Lusaka, where they were proclaimed.

At the time of the reforms, almost all businesses were owned and operated by people of either Asian or European origin. Many of the Asians had come to Zambia after World War II, during the copper boom, because they saw the chance to improve life for themselves and their families by setting up shops. Most of them did well.

When Independence came, all foreign residents of Zambia

were invited to take out Zambian citizenship, but only if they would give up any other citizenship they had claim to. Many of the Asian people held British passports as Commonwealth citizens and did not want to let them go. Only 298 out of over 10,000 Asians became Zambian citizens between 1965 and 1971. During this same time no more than 630 Europeans out of between 50,000 and 70,000 received citizenship.

The economic reforms were not intended to affect those who were citizens, African or not. After the reforms were announced, there was a flood of applications for citizenship, but very, very few were granted; the Zambian government felt that those who applied only to stay in business had no real commitment to Zambia and her ideals.

The plight of the Asians, not only in Zambia, but in Tanzania, Kenya, and Uganda as well, has been a complicated and many-sided one. Asians tended to monopolize certain types of businesses such as grocery stores, drug stores, and shoe shops. The Asians, mostly from India, kept very much to themselves during their years in Africa. They conducted business efficiently, but very often with a hostility toward the Africans. No attempt at all was made to include Africans in their businesses. It was understandable why Zambia wanted to change this situation after Independence.

On the other hand, when the Asians were forced to give up their businesses, many had nowhere to go. Great Britain imposed immigration quotas on non-English passport holders; India refused to accept most of them back. Zambia put a strict limit on how much money emigrants could take away. Many Asian families went from a position of comfort to one of poverty and homelessness.

The government asked that the Asians turn over their businesses to Africans. In some cases this happened; in others, the shops were simply closed, either because there was no African with the capital to buy the business or because the Asians made no effort to find one. When possible, the state-owned Industrial Development Corporation (INDECO) either took over a business or lent the money to a Zambian to acquire it, but this was not always feasible. Closing down shops in rural areas placed a burden, at least temporarily, on the Africans who had no other source of supply.

After the Mulungushi Reforms, the Zambian government started participating more and more actively in the economy. INDECO, acting for the government, took over a number of large industries. In most cases, this meant that INDECO would own 51 percent of the shares in the business or industry and could thus control its policies when necessary, but private ownership of the other 49 percent was allowed. There are some corporations which are 100 percent state-owned. This policy differs from that in the United States, where the government can try to influence businesses and industries but does not actually own them. President Kaunda and his advisors saw government takeover of industry and commerce as the only way in which the Zambian economy could be developed on a systematic basis, in a way to benefit all Zambians and not just a privileged few. In industries regulated by the government, Zambianization could be much more rapid.

The industries obtained by the government had been owned and operated by foreigners. Asians had been the owners of small businesses, but Europeans were most affected by the takeover of industry. The Zambian government promised to pay for the amount taken. So far, the government has stood behind its pledges, and foreign investors are continuing to come to Zambia despite the policy of government control.

In 1969, Kaunda dramatically announced a similar takeover, or nationalization, of 51 percent of the mines. (In addition to copper, zinc, lead, coal, and small amounts of limestone, amethyst, emeralds, and tin are mined in Zambia.) A takeover of the mines had seemed almost inevitable; the government wanted control over its main source of revenue. MINDECO was set up to administer the government shares of the mines, although a government ministry assumed the role in 1973. FINDECO was created to oversee financial institutions run by the government. The National Transport Corporation and the National Hotels Corporation were the fourth and fifth bodies formed to look after state interests. In April 1974, the National Energy Corporation became the sixth government company.

ZIMCO (Zambia Industrial and Mining Corporation) is the central company, spreading like an umbrella over all six state corporations just named. President Kaunda is chairman of the board of ZIMCO. ZIMCO is one of the world's largest organizations with an aftertax profit of $147,502,600 in 1971. In 1973, ZIMCO won the "International Trophy for Industry," awarded by the International Institute for Promotion and Prestige. The recognition was for ZIMCO's "contribution to improving the life of the people of Zambia." No other African business organization has ever won this award.

During the first six years of independence, a new industry was started in Zambia on an average of every fourth working day. Zambia has gone from a country with virtually no industries, dependent upon importing almost everything, to a country with a wide and growing variety of commercial concerns. Among the multitude of products from the new manufacturing plants are glass bottles, made with local sand and Kenya soda ash; wire mesh; fertilizer; cloth from Zambian cotton; processed tea; refined sugar; records; plastics; beer; furniture; and matches. Zambia has obtained loans from foreign countries to aid her in starting most of her new industries, but at least they are locally controlled and provide employment for Zambians. Especially with Zambia's transportation difficulties, it is much better than depending so heavily on imports.

To become self-sufficient is the goal in agriculture, as well as industry. Far back in the history of the Zambian tribes, agriculture was never an occupation with much prestige. During the colonial days, Africans were discouraged from competing with European farmers in the country. Nonetheless, a full three-fourths of the Zambian people live in rural areas and participate in farming of some sort.

By 1972, Zambian farms were producing enough maize (corn), sugar, groundnuts (peanuts), chickens, and eggs for the nation's needs. It may be several years before Zambia has enough of her other staple foods such as beef, vegetable oils, fruits, coffee,

Record pressing, one of Zambia's new industries.

tea, and rice. The swampy conditions of Luapula Province are perfect for rice growing, and a large scheme sponsored by the French is under way there. When it is fully developed, there may be as many as seven thousand rice farmers.

Important cash crops, sold either within or outside the country, include maize, cassava, poultry, beef, groundnuts, tobacco, sugar, and cotton. Although the Southern and Central provinces have traditionally been the biggest farming areas, almost all the tobacco and groundnuts, both of very high quality, are grown in Eastern Province.

What is agriculture like in Zambia? Large-scale farming on an individual basis is not possible; the most land any one person can own is twenty-five acres. Farms, then, are either very small, usually producing just enough for a single family or village, or are part of a cooperative scheme or a government project. The government encourages cooperatives as a part of Zambian Humanism. The Rural Development Corporation (RDC) was set up in 1968 to plan, supervise, and coordinate large agricultural projects and to encourage the establishment of new agricultural industries. RDC has also worked in the area of pest control and eradication.

Fish is one of the staple foods of Zambia. Fishermen, as well as farmers, are learning modern techniques of their trade, and output is increasing.

Developing the rural areas and erasing the differences in standards of living, services, and opportunities between cities and the rest of the country have been aims of all Zambian planning since Independence. But these goals had a special place in the Second

The Mukonchi tobacco growers' scheme, one of the giant agricultural developments in Zambia.

National Development Plan (SNDP), covering the years 1972 to 1976. Under this plan special Intensive Development Zones (IDZ) were chosen. The IDZ are places where the soil is good, which are close to transport of some sort, and which generally show promise for successful output. Although these sites were slated for concentrated development, all rural land is included in improvement plans. The government wants to cut food imports, provide raw materials for Zambian industry, and raise rural incomes. INDECO is also setting up new industries in more remote sections of Zambia. The new roads and railroads make this possible.

Zambian planners work out development plans by estimating what the revenue of the country will be during the time a plan covers, what the goals of the country are for that period, and how the money available should be spent to obtain those goals. At best, the plans establish priorities and provide a general direction in which the country tries to move. Unexpected events such as UDI in 1965 and the border closure in 1973 cause major shifting of revenue, and income is really unpredictable, especially with the fluctuation of copper prices.

Although transportation facilities will not be increased as much under the SNDP as they were just after UDI, there are plans for continued paving of roads. The United States has approved over $840,000 for a major four-hundred-mile highway to Botswana; Zambia obtains beef from this country to the south and frequently it has had to be airlifted in. The Chinese are constructing a road to Mongu in the Western Province; this road should decrease the feeling of separateness that the people of this province have traditionally felt.

An improved transport network is essential for successful agricultural development. For example, after the total ban on the import of South African fruits and vegetables in 1970, several farmers increased their output, only to discover that the government could not buy their products because of transport and storage difficulties.

Zambia's airport facilities are the star of her transportation system. When the Lusaka International Airport was opened in

1967, it was the second largest in Africa. All sizes of jets, including the 747, can land there. With help from Alitalia Airlines, Zambia Airways was established in 1967. The airline has been rapidly Zambianized and has international flights to other countries and to Europe as well as domestic service with Zambia.

On December 2, 1972, in what has become known as the "Kabwe Declaration," Kaunda announced a very strict Leadership Code. The point of the Leadership Code is to keep persons in high positions, be they political, military, or industrial leaders, from using their offices to accumulate personal wealth. No such person can draw more than one salary; he can either work for the government without salary or give up whatever other source of income he might have. He cannot hold rental property while living in a government house. He cannot be a director in a private company. In June 1974, some modifications of the code were announced that somewhat softened the harshness of the regulations, but the main thrust of the code is the same. This Leadership Code and many of Zambia's other reforms were patterned after actions taken by President Nyerere of the neighboring country of Tanzania.

A country's economy, of course, cannot operate without a means of payment. The monetary unit in Zambia, the *kwacha,* was introduced in 1968. Until this time, the British pound was the basis of the currency. A kwacha is equal to $1.40. The kwacha is broken up into one hundred units, just as our dollar is. Each unit is an *ngwee. Kwacha* means "dawn" or "freedom" and *ngwee* means "brightness is coming"; both were rallying cries during the fight for independence.

Traditionally, money trading in Zambia was done under the shade of the *mutaba* (fig) tree. Banking in Zambia is now modern and efficient. Recently, the method of saving money at the post office savings bank, a leftover from the British period, has ceased and savings are kept at a national savings bank.

Clearly Zambia has taken giant steps toward the goal of independence from a "borrowed fiddle." The Zambian people are being educated to make the best use of the expanding resources available to them.

13

A Will to Learn

Prior to Independence, the responsibility for African education was left to a large extent in the hands of the mines and the missions. The missions still manage some primary schools funded by the government, contribute a small percentage of costs for secondary education, and help to recruit teachers. The mines continue to promote and support education for their employees. However, the lion's share of the task of education now rests squarely on the shoulders of the Zambian government.

A quick look at the state of education in 1964 reveals the formidable task the government had to assume. The need for educated Zambians was acute. Zambia achieved independence with only one hundred college graduates, twelve hundred high school graduates, and six thousand additional persons who had finished even two years of high school. Primary education in Zambia compared favorably with that in other African countries at their times of Independence, but, even so, fewer than half the children between five and fourteen were in school. Nearly two-thirds of the adult population could neither read nor write.

Zambia's arrival at independence with so few educated citizens was not a result of economic necessity. The revenue from copper created a continually fat treasury, and much more could have been spent on school development. At best, the colonial government had simply thought education unimportant for Africans. At worst, the Europeans deliberately neglected African education to prevent competition for jobs. In a desperate attempt to catch up, the Zambian government spent four times as much on education during the six years after Independence as the British had in the preceding forty years.

Until Independence, fees were required for all schooling. Since then, the majority of schools have become free. Only the former European institutions, where places are in the greatest demand, still charge fees. Some primary and most secondary students are boarders. Students are purposely sent by the government to parts of the country other than their own to help create more feeling of national unity.

English is the official language for all classes, though this decree is not strictly followed in the most remote rural areas, where almost no children come to school speaking English. Students whose parents are frequently transferred find adjusting to new schools much easier now that they no longer face the possibility of having to learn a new language with each move.

Most elementary schools are coeducational, but high schools are usually divided according to sex. More than twice as many boys as girls attend school; at the university level, there are seven times as many.

The whole country became involved in expanding educational facilities after Independence. Self-help schemes spread through the rural areas. The government provided villagers with materials for erecting school buildings in return for their labor. By this method over 2,000 classrooms with places for 120,000 students were built in a period of two years. Shortly after Independence, in an urban area, the Copperbelt, a day was set aside called *Ubushiku bwa Kwafwana,* "the day for helping each other." On that day, every child was asked to contribute approximately sixty-five cents to a furniture fund for schools. Other, less satisfactory ways to meet demands have also been used—double and triple sessions and extremely overcrowded classrooms.

Each year a higher percentage of Zambian children enter primary school, but because of the severe shortage of places in upper primary and secondary schools, a smaller and smaller percentage can actually go on through the school system.

Under the Second National Development Plan, the government hopes that primary education will be available for every

Outdoor play at a rural Zambian primary school.

child through fourth grade and for 80 percent of the population in the upper three primary grades. A severe problem is population growth. Zambia has one of the fastest growing populations in the world. More than half the population is under twenty-five years of age; 46 percent is under fifteen. The need for new classrooms is constant.

Overcrowding in the early grades has been even worse than the government anticipated because it is impossible to determine who is old enough to start Grade I. Although the legal age for entering school in Zambia is seven (except for fee-paying schools, where it is five), five- or six-year-olds are often passed off as seven. Because parents generally do not register the births of their children, the school has no birth certificate to check the correct age of a child. Celebrating birthdays has never been a custom among Zambians. Frequently, an adult does not know his age or birthdate.

In Zambian schools, there are seven primary grades and five years of high school. Students are selected out by examination after fourth and seventh grade and after Form (grade) II and IV in high school. Some students who have passed the exam are dropped simply because there is not enough room.

The World Bank is funding an Educational Project in Zambia that was begun in the early 1970s. A large part of the loan is for building new secondary schools, remodeling old ones, and expanding school equipment. There is no hope for everyone in Zambia, or for that matter in most African countries, to have a high school education before the end of this century. The price is too high even for a nation greatly concerned with education. The goal now is simply to keep pace with the country's needs for graduates. Many Africans feel this should continue to be the goal. High school education for all is seen as a frill in a land of poverty.

The Zambian government is striving for quality, as well as quantity, in education. A new primary plan emphasizes active rather than passive learning. "New math" and other curriculum changes have been introduced.

The 60 or 70 percent of Zambian young people who have no place in secondary school become "school-leavers" at the end of seventh grade. Although one does not have to be ashamed of being a school-leaver, so many persons who are too young or too unskilled to work creates a major social problem.

In 1968, J. M. Mwanakatwe, a former minister of education in Zambia, wrote a book entitled *The Growth of Education in Zambia since Independence*. In the book, he suggests that young people be prepared before they leave school to return to and make a living from the land. Although it does not seem as glamorous as some other careers, a rural life is the only solution for the majority of the population.

Some school-leavers are recruited for the National Service, known until 1971 as the Zambia Youth Service. All members must study agriculture. However, there are additional training courses available and on-the-job experience for those who succeed. Since 1971, the emphasis has seemed to shift from agriculture to defense. The youths in the service learn to use light weapons and serve as an additional force ready to defend their country.

Vocational and technical training schools provide yet another alternative to school-leavers. Prevocational courses, bringing students to the level of Form II, are offered in many trade schools.

Some career programs require some high school work; others require graduation. The Northern Technical College at Ndola, the Zambia Institute of Technology at Kitwe and Luanshya, and the Evelyn Hone College of Applied Arts and Commerce at Lusaka are three of the major institutions offering training for mechanics, accountants, engineers, architects, health technicians, secretaries, bookkeepers, pharmacists, and numerous other occupations. Many industries and businesses cooperate in providing education for their recruits. The National Institute for Public Administration at Lusaka is a school for government workers.

In March 1966, the doors of the University of Zambia were opened. President Kaunda, the chancellor, wept openly at the ceremonies. It was a time of deep emotion for many Zambians. The university was a symbol to them of all their country had lacked and might now have. From throughout the land, rich and poor alike contributed generously to a fund-raising drive.

Zambia is already educating her own lawyers, doctors, engineers, and teachers, although it will be some years before the university has reached its capacity of five thousand full-time students.

Lying in the midst of rolling, green hills, surrounded by lakes, palm trees, and flowers, the university seems a peaceful oasis. Like universities around the world, however, it has not been without its times of turmoil. In August 1971, the university was

The University of Zambia.

temporarily closed and ten members of the Student Executive Committee were permanently expelled.

The incident centered around Zambia's relations with the racist governments to her south, as have so many events in her recent history. Students staged a demonstration at the French Embassy against France's building of Mirage jets in South Africa. Black Africans see a great danger in any military buildup in South Africa; they feel the purpose of weapons is to further suppress the rights of black South Africans. Police broke up the demonstrations and one student was shot. The protest continued with an open letter to President Kaunda, critical of his dealings in the South African matter. The students who were expelled had signed the letter.

Adult education centers have sprung up throughout the country since Independence. Immediately after Independence, the fervent desire of many adults was to become literate, so most courses were in the basic skills of reading and writing. Now the emphasis has shifted to high school subjects and vocational training. In 1967, the two major mining companies contributed over $540,000 to adult education classes, which were opened to private citizens as well as to mine employees. This money was for use in courses other than those specifically designed to train employees for promotion.

A very logical problem to arise from such a rapid expansion of education at all levels, for all ages, is a critical need for teachers. In 1970, in Zambia, 13 percent of the primary school teachers had no training except their own primary school education. Most elementary school teachers are Zambians, but in 1970 only one out of every ten secondary teachers was a Zambian. The other 90 percent were recruited from countries all over the world.

Under the World Bank Project, teacher training institutions are being expanded. Students who have finished two years of high school are accepted for a one- or two-year primary teacher training course. The course for secondary teachers is two years and there are plans to lengthen it to three. High school graduates or experienced teachers can apply for this program. There is also a school of education at the university.

The teacher shortage is equally severe at the university level. Although the number of African scholars on the faculty is steadily increasing, the great majority of professors come from more than thirty countries outside Zambia. The cost of importing so many teachers is prohibitive.

Libraries at the university and for the public have backed up the education drive in Zambia. The university library, opened in 1969, has 230,000 volumes. The Zambia Library Service was founded in 1960 and funded by the Ford Foundation of New York. The goal of the service is to provide free library facilities throughout the country.

Educational radio and television also supplement classroom instruction. Zambia's Educational Broadcasting Service won a special prize in 1966 and again in 1967 at an international educational broadcasting competition held in Tokyo. So far, TV broadcasts have gone to schools in Lusaka and on the Copperbelt. Radio receivers are less expensive and more widely distributed.

Zambia hopes to solve many of her problems through the educational system. She has done well in regard to goals set for all

African nations at a UNESCO conference on education held during the 1960s in Ethiopia, and especially well in comparison to where she was in 1964 and in contrast to neighboring countries. But the funds are limited, the need is greater than can easily be remedied, and the work has just begun.

14

Toward a Healthier Nation

A sick body, or one that is weak with hunger, usually contains a mind that is too tired to concentrate or to care about learning. Good education, then, is of little use without good health.

The European's type of education has been easier for many Africans to accept than his health care systems. Traditional African education helped a child to understand his life and to live it creatively and productively; modern education has the same goal, just a different means of reaching it. On the other hand, many aspects of traditional health care have been intertwined with superstitions, clouded by the power of witchcraft, and darkened by emotion. Magic potions continue to work for some people who believe strongly enough that they will. It is widely accepted that germs cause illnesses. But the reason one person gets a germ and another does not might be attributed to actions of the local witch doctor. As one old Bemba teacher said, "It is unfortunate that the magic of the African and the science of the white man do not work together. Neither alone is as strong as the combination could be."

Despite the vast needs, the demands on resources, and the psychological obstacles, Zambia moves steadily forward in the field of health care. Governmental efforts reach in every direction: toward building new facilities, training the personnel for them, and helping each Zambian break down any barriers of fear or misunderstanding he may have.

Health care is free for everyone. In this sense, the average Zambian is better taken care of than the average American. The number of diseases to be battled, however, is far greater than in the United States. Certain diseases are confined to areas with tropical conditions, among them malaria, bilharziasis, leprosy, and sleeping sickness. Others originated in more temperate climates and were brought to Zambia by outsiders. The Africans have dreaded the diseases imported by the white man as much as the settlers have stood in fear of those they discovered in Zambia.

Malaria is currently a prime target of attack in the health program. The word malaria means "bad air," and for many years men believed that breathing the air above the African swamps caused the disease. Approximately seventy years ago, the mosquito was identified as the carrier of the malaria parasite. The parasite lives in and destroys red blood cells. The victim has chills followed by high fever and anemia. Some types of malaria occur again and again in a single person. In Zambia over twenty thousand people are admitted to the hospital each year with malaria. Children are especially susceptible to the disease.

Lusaka has had few cases of malaria in recent years, but there are other parts of the country where it is difficult to escape. A survey of the Northern Province in 1970 found 30 percent of the people infected with malaria. The lower-lying, more swampy parts of the country are breeding grounds for the malaria-carrying mosquitoes. Even the urban areas of the Copperbelt have had a recent rise in malaria.

The beautiful rivers and lakes of Africa are often deceptive in appearance. Beneath their surface lurks the carrier of the bilharzia, a tiny flatworm that, like the malaria parasite, infects the blood. Bilharzia enters the water from human waste. Its host in the water is a snail in which part of the life cycle of the bilharzia takes place. A person drinking, bathing or swimming, or washing clothes in water where the snails live can become infected. The bilharzia attacks the intestines, bladder, liver, spleen, and other vital organs. The illness can last for long periods of time, causing a person to become weaker and weaker. In Zambia attempts are being made to eliminate the snail, especially in Lake

Kariba, but, so far, they have not met with much success. Clean water supplies are a must for good health.

Trypanosomiasis or sleeping sickness is no longer prevalent in Zambia but has had a profound effect on events in the past. Men and animals are both affected by this deadly disease. Particularly significant to Zambia's history is the fact that cattle cannot live where the disease exists. Cattle-keeping tribes, therefore, could settle only in areas free of the tsetse fly, the carrier of the organism which causes sleeping sickness.

Since biblical times, leprosy has been known as a dread disease, causing infected persons to become outcasts from society. This is no longer necessary because if leprosy is treated in its earliest stages, it can be converted into a noncontagious disease and a victim can live normally. In 1972, in Zambia, there were only 1,700 patients living permanently in leper colonies, although there were 4.43 known cases of leprosy per 1,000 population, a total of approximately 17,000.

Zambia, lying on the high plateau, escapes the severity of tropical diseases that exist in many other parts of Africa, particularly the rain forests of West Africa, which were known in the nineteenth century as the "white man's grave." Yellow fever is one tropical disease that does not occur in Zambia at all.

Smallpox is another disease that disappeared in 1969. Zambian health officials launched an enormous inoculation campaign just after Independence, and Zambia became the first among neighboring countries to completely eliminate smallpox. It is now nonexistent in most countries of the world. The World Health Organization, which Zambia joined in 1965, aided the smallpox eradication program and supports many other health projects in Zambia.

Neither measles, one of the most dreaded diseases for children at the present time, nor tuberculosis, nor polio is the worst nontropical killer introduced by European civilization. More hospital admissions and deaths are the result of automobile accidents. The accident rate on the line-of-rail between Lusaka and the Copperbelt is one of the highest in the world. It is so high, in fact, that car rental firms charge almost twice as much as the airlines to cover that distance.

Perhaps most pitiful of all illnesses in Africa are those caused by inadequate diet. Not only do these diseases create their own problems, but they also make the person much more susceptible to every other type of sickness.

Marasmus and kwashiorkor are common malnutrition diseases. They attack children, usually those under five. Marasmus is caused by lack of food in general. The child suffering from it is literally starving to death. He becomes extremely thin and

Many Zambian children must scrape the pot to find even a few scraps of food.

weak, but with a very distended stomach. Kwashiorkor is caused by lack of protein. In addition to stunted growth, a sufferer will have swollen legs and feet, a change in skin and hair color, and muscles which don't develop properly.

A child with either marasmus or kwashiorkor can be spotted easily. He can also be cured, except in the most severe stages, by the introduction of the proper foods into his diet.

Often children are affected by these diseases of malnutrition because their parents do not understand the relationship between diet and good health. The death rate for children under five is 40 to 50 percent of those born. An additional 20 percent suffer from malnutrition. Furthermore, Zambian custom dictates that men eat first, then women, and finally children. In a poor family, there is frequently nothing left by the children's turn.

Superstitions such as the one that says a woman who eats eggs will become pregnant are still widely believed. The Zambian government realizes the need for education and improved nutrition and works through its agency, the National Food and Nutrition Commission. Many words of praise can be said for the work done by this commission, which was unique on the continent of Africa when it began. It has been so thorough and successful that many other African nations are seeking advice on establishing similar programs.

One of the most successful programs of the Food and Nutrition Commission has been the under-five clinics. The national goal is to have such a clinic at each health unit throughout the country. Mothers can bring their children to these clinics weekly or monthly to be weighed and to receive vaccinations. Signs of improper feeding can be spotted early and mothers can be assisted in learning the methods to correct it. Under-five clinics originated in Nigeria, but now Zambia has more than any other African nation.

As far away as the streets of Nairobi, Kenya, one can see posters, prepared by the National Food and Nutrition Commission, encouraging African women to breast-feed their babies. Patterning after many Europeans, and influenced by high-pressure salesmanship, a great many African women have abandoned

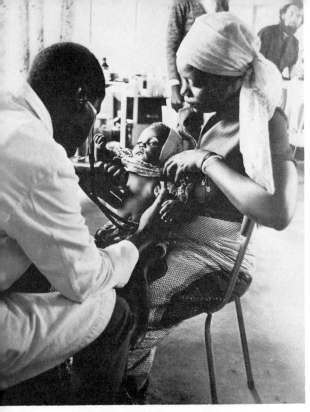

A medical assistant examines
a baby at an under-five clinic.

breast-feeding for the more expensive and frequently more dangerous method of bottle-feeding. Often bottles of milk are not
properly washed or refrigerated. As the poster emphasizes,
mothers who do breast-feed, in addition, need to know when to
introduce solid foods or malnutrition will occur. The belief has
been widespread that nursing without supplement is sufficient
until a child is four or five years old.

A fruitful project started by individual initiative is the Lusaka
Nutrition Group. Under the direction of an Anglican priest, vol-
unteers from churches of many denominations and several other
groups set up sixty food depots in Lusaka. These were
frequently in homes. At the depots, the staple and basically nutritious foods of the country—kapenta (fish), beans, milk powder
—are sold at lower than retail prices. Lectures and demonstrations on good nutrition, proper cooking, etc., are given to the

patrons of the depots and much emphasis here, too, is placed on the health of mothers and children. Mealiemeal (cornmeal) mixed with water into a dish known as *nshima* is the staple diet of many Zambians. It is starchy and filling but not nutritious. The demonstrations at the depots emphasize mixing a protein-rich food with the nshima. Between 1967 and 1971, the number of depots grew to six hundred and spread from Lusaka into many rural areas.

Nutrition clubs exist at schools throughout Zambia. Members learn about and practice good nutrition, sharing their findings with the entire student body of their schools.

Good nutrition helps prevent disease, but, for those who do become ill, the desperate need remains for more trained doctors, nurses, and other medical personnel and for more health facilities of every kind. In 1972, there were 425 doctors, one for every 9,500 inhabitants, compared to one doctor in America for every 585 people. In the same year, Zambia had 122 hygiene teachers, 1,800 nurses, and 195 midwives. Peppered across the country are clinics, small six-bed rural health centers, larger centers, and over seventy-five hospitals. The new teaching hospital at the University of Zambia hopes to have more than 1,200 beds. The aim is to have no one more than a few miles from at least a health center within fifteen to twenty years. Again the government has taken responsibility for a function that used to be left to the missions and the mines.

For those Zambians who are now too far from even a clinic to receive treatment, there is the Flying Doctor Service. In 1968, there were nine remote airstrip clinics, visited two or three times weekly by a medical orderly. Serious cases are evacuated. The missions also provide air medical service. Motorboats equipped as clinics are used to reach fishermen in isolated water regions. These services are decreasing as other facilities become available.

Zambian medical personnel are steadily replacing those recruited from abroad. Between sixteen and twenty-five doctors will graduate each year from the University of Zambia, and five or six dental students are sent abroad to study each year. The numbers of sisters (nurses), midwives, and health instructors are increasing also. Medical assistants make the shortage of doctors less critical. They receive three years of training and can diagnose and treat diseases as well as work at preventing them. Located in a suburb of Lusaka is the Reference Health Center, which provides training and a model for health center personnel at new facilities.

Birth control is a controversial issue in Zambia, as in many African countries. Some Zambians believe that unchecked population growth is acceptable, even desirable, in a rapidly expanding economy. Others, however, think control of family size is necessary in order to raise the standard of living and to prevent a strain on the social services the government is trying to provide. The Zambian government has not forbidden birth control but is not actively educating in this area. Health officials, however, encourage mothers to space their children to protect their own well-being.

The life expectancy in America is 71 years. In Zambia, it is 38.9. This figure alone reveals the enormous need for every effort the Zambian government makes to create a healthier nation.

15

Customs and Culture

On both the flag of Zambia and her coat of arms there appears an eagle. Traditionally an eagle has represented freedom and strength. Yet another meaning for Zambia's eagle might be found in a parable written down by a West African, James Aggrey. He uses the parable to explain the colonial experience of most Africans.

As he tells it, a certain man found a young eagle, took it home, and raised it among ducks, turkeys, and chickens as if it were one of them. After several years a naturalist traveling through the area spotted the bird. The naturalist insisted that, although the eagle had never been taught to fly, its inborn ability would enable it to. The farmer maintained that it had been told for so long that it was a chicken that it could never fly. After several unsuccessful attempts, the eagle suddenly stretched forth its wings and soared away, never to return. Aggrey ends his parable with these words:

> My people of Africa, we were created in the image of God, but men have made us think that we are chickens, and we still think we are; but we are eagles. Stretch forth your wings and fly! Don't be content with the food of chickens! *

* Reprinted in Leon E. Clark, ed., *Through African Eyes* (New York: Praeger, 1969), p. 485.

Since Independence, Zambians have tried to regain a sense of dignity and self-worth, to once again be "eagles" rather than "chickens."

Although Zambians agree on their goals of self-esteem and pride in their culture, there are disagreements as to how to realize these goals. A controversy rages between those who feel any and all customs adopted from the Europeans should be abandoned and those who believe that modern ways are better than the old and should be followed. The moderate position lies somewhere in between, with those who treasure traditional African culture and want it preserved, yet believe that the good aspects of other cultures can be a benefit. Regardless of which view one supports, the fact remains that Zambian life in the last quarter of the twentieth century can be most accurately described as a melange of the old and the new, of traditional African and contemporary Western culture.

Some old customs that have survived have been modified. Initiation ceremonies, for example, frequently take place during one weekend—perhaps when the young person is home from boarding school—rather than over an extended period of several weeks. The lobola is one of the most lasting traditions, but since the introduction of the European monetary system, the traditional gifts have largely been replaced by cash. Polygamy is no more frequent than it ever was, but it is practiced by some. The most frequent example is a man who has one wife in the village, his "bush wife," and another in the city where he works.

Traditional dancing is still an integral part of modern life, but its purpose is not always what it was in the past. The dances that once accompanied initiations—and in some areas continue to—or welcomed returning warriors after a kill, now greet visiting dignitaries at the airport or provide entertainment at state banquets. The Zambian National Dance Troupe works long and hard hours; most traditional dances require endless practice and skill. The *Vimbuza* of the Timbuka society in eastern Zambia and the *Makishi* are two of the most popular traditional dances in modern Zambia.

The *Kalela* is a unique nontraditional dance, which grew up on

A dancer from the Zambian National Dance Troupe, accompanied by drums.

the Copperbelt. It is performed by members of one tribe who imitate and/or poke fun at another tribe. Often the men who participate are dressed in Western business suits rather than in African dress.

The instruments most commonly used to accompany the traditional dances are drums; the *mbira,* or thumb piano, a wooden board or box over which strips of metal or bamboo of varying lengths are tied; xylophones, flutes, horns, rattles, and bells. The latter two are often attached to the dancers' arms or legs. Drums come in many shapes and sizes; some are played with sticks, others by hand. The *Vimbuza* dance is accomplished by three drums; the *Nyau* of the Chewa, by five. The slow, steady beating of an African drum, sometimes for hours on end, once heard, is not soon forgotten. Sounds from the various African instruments, mingled with the sometimes mournful singing tones, blend together in a rich mixture of rhythm and pitch.

Cultural exchange between Zambia and the rest of the world has not been a one-way transaction with Zambia always incorporating elements of a foreign culture into her own. Rather, ideas have flowed in both directions. For example, the rhythms and instruments of African music have made their way into the music of Europe and America. In return, there are Western-type combo bands in Zambia. A well-known Copperbelt group of the early 1970s is the Fireballs.

The Rising Stars is a unique group of very young musicians who have traveled throughout Zambia, the rest of Africa, and Europe giving performances. They are present at almost every occasion of importance in Zambia, singing and playing the accordion, the melodia (an accordionlike wind instrument), tambourines, triangles, drums, and the string bass.

A Zambian artist working on a carving.

Elements of African art have also found their place in the modern art of the West. Picasso was one grand master who was profoundly influenced by what he observed in African art. In Zambia, as elsewhere in Africa, painting has not been a common form of artistic expression. Wood sculpture, pottery making, and basket weaving are the customary crafts. Only recently have some Zambian artists branched out into the two-dimensional world on canvas. The Nchanga Consolidated Mines sponsor an annual painting contest for Zambian students and use the winning pictures on a calendar.

In Zambia, many beautiful stories and poems have been handed down orally for countless generations, but literature in written form is an entirely new element of culture for Zambians. Some authors have attempted to transfer the style of the oral traditions to their written works. Without the inflections of the voice and the language of the body used in verbal literature, their words often fall flat. The art and drama of the traditional stories can be conveyed in written form, but the impact is lost when the tales are transcribed verbatim without the motions and intonations represented by words.

Seminars sponsored by the university and by literary societies are held to encourage the creation of a Zambian literature and to discuss the problems facing Zambian writers. Most controversial among the problems is whether the authors will write in English or in their tribal language. So far, in Zambia, most of the writing of fiction has been in African languages. Several novels written in Bemba, Tonga, Lozi, and Nyanja have appeared. In 1971, the first two major novels written in English by Zambians were published. One was *Before Dawn,* written by Andreya Masiye. The other novel, *Tongue of the Dumb,* was written by Dominic Mulaisho. He was the first Zambian to have a work of fiction included in the internationally recognized Heinemann's African Writers Series. Kenneth Kaunda's autobiography, *Zambia Shall Be Free,* is also a part of the series.

Which language to speak, as well as which language to write, is a serious question to many Zambians. English is now the only official language. The arguments for English are that it has a large, more scientific, and internationally known vocabulary, more books are available, and, if English is used, the language of no one tribe is given preference over that of another. Proponents of an African language fear that soon the African languages, and thus an important part of African culture, will disappear. They suggest introducing an "outside" African language such as Swahili while expanding the vocabulary of existing languages. If a trend toward writing in English continues to develop, the chance for the growth of the African languages is minimized.

At present all the major periodic and news publications in Zambia are in English. For daily news coverage, there is *The Times of Zambia* or the government-owned *Zambia Mail*. Due to transportation limitations, until the early 1970s these newspapers circulated mainly along the line-of-rail. *Z Magazine* (z is pronounced "zed" in Zambia), put out by the Zambia Information Services, provides a means for Zambians and non-Zambians alike to keep up with the current events in Zambia in culture, business, sport, and government. *Orbit* is a colorful, well-prepared, serious, yet entertaining magazine for Zambian young people. Puzzles and games, how-to-do-it instructions, crafts, hobbies, stories in comic strip form, biographies of famous Zambians, nature studies, tips on science, farming, and sports news are only a few of the varied features. The main publications for those who do not speak or read English are newssheets published in local languages by the Zambia Information Service. The news coverage is not detailed and it does not appear daily.

Whether Zambian women should wear Western-style clothes or "traditional dress," the long skirts adopted when the missionaries first arrived, is a point of conflict among some of the people. In some African countries, very short skirts have been banned. On occasion, in Zambia, members of the National Service have stopped women in the street and with scissors and knives have lowered the hems of dresses they felt inappropriately short. Above-the-knee skirts are not forbidden in Zambia, but Zambian women are encouraged to wear the *chitenge,* a piece of material wrapped around the body to form a long skirt. Many young girls find these skirts cumbersome and confining

Zambian women dressed in *chitenge*.

for everyday wear. Zambian women are also pressured not to wear long pants or shorts. Somehow it is considered much more acceptable for men to wear contemporary Western fashions than it is for women.

An extremely appealing outfit worn by Zambian women is created when a dress and a high turban-type headpiece are made from the same colorful, patterned material. The headpieces are worn with both long and short skirts.

Women in Zambia are becoming more and more conscious of their positions vis-a-vis men. As is the case in the United States, there are some who prefer to accept the traditional role of the woman in the home and some who wish to enter the career world on an equal footing with men. In rural areas, most women still maintain their traditional attitudes, but in the cities, many women, including those who do not work, are beginning to seek a more respected position.

Until very recently, Zambian women were barred from most higher education and most jobs, even from those meager opportunities that were available to African men. They have had to seek liberation from discrimination because of both race and sex. In 1970 and 1971, there were articles in *Z Magazine* on the first woman state lawyer and the first woman postmaster in Zambia. In December 1973, President Kaunda appointed a woman solicitor-general. It was the first time a woman had held such a high office in Africa. One area in which Zambian women have excelled is sports. In January 1973, the second All-Africa Games, similar to the Olympics, were held in Lagos, Nigeria. The Zambian delegation was the only one with more women than men. When asked about this, one young woman athlete said, "Oh, the boys failed to qualify." Unfortunately, there are many fields where the first woman has been accepted only very recently . . . or not yet.

Discipline for children has always been quite strict. Children are expected to be obedient and completely respectful to every older person. Their rights are few until they are initiated into the adult world. On the other hand, a Zambian child usually spends a large number of hours each day without any adult supervision. During this time, he is freer than children in many societies.

The daily life of the majority of Zambian children is very different from that of most American children. The following description appears in the book *Children in Zambia* by Edith Dahlschen.* Zambian children, she says, learn to

> pound, to draw water, to look after babies and cattle, to do garden work and field work in a playful way. They

* Lusaka: National Educational Company of Zambia, Ltd., 1972.

produce their own toys, which are imitations of articles from the adult world. Their games and pastimes are directed by realistic needs. They fish and hunt small animals, gather fruit and wild vegetables. They improvise their own songs on any subject, as they have learnt from their elders.

There are some children, of course, who live "city lives," just as there are some American children who grow up close to nature like the Zambian children described above.

In traditional days, a Zambian child went directly from childhood to the assumption of adult responsibilities. Western culture and longer schooling have introduced the concept of adolescence. Zambian young people are now faced with this period in which they are sexually mature but socially unprepared for adulthood.

Sports are popular in Zambia with both children and adults. The national sport is soccer, or football (both terms are used by Zambians). Soccer stars are heroes, just as football, baseball, and basketball stars are in the United States. The national soccer season lasts for eight months.

Another game played by boys, similar to American football, is rugby. The American game, in fact, was derived from rugby and soccer. Cricket is a popular sport played with a bat and ball and two eleven-man teams. American baseball is a stepchild of cricket. Field hockey is played by both boys and girls, but net ball, somewhat like basketball, is considered a girls' sport.

Bowls (bowling), tennis, golf, squash, badminton, swimming, and horseback riding are enjoyed by Zambians, and recently basketball and volleyball have become popular. Bicycling and fishing are widespread but not as sports so much as necessary parts of daily life.

Most sports in Zambia were borrowed from the British colonial society, but there is one very well liked game which has been played for many centuries and is exclusively African. It goes by many names. In Zambia, as in other countries, it is called something different by each tribe. One Zambian name for it is *chisolo*.

President Kaunda congratulates the winners of a soccer match.

The game is played on a board with carved-out holes or pockets. Each of the two participants starts with a certain number of playing pieces and attempts to capture those of his opponent. The skill demanded of a good chess player is needed to be a frequent winner.

Radio and, for the wealthier Zambians, TV are other current forms of entertainment. "Zamarts" is a locally produced television program which was started to promote Zambian culture. It has been criticized for limiting itself to traditional dancing rather than incorporating other art forms. Zambian-made quiz and news broadcasts appear as well as programs imported from other countries, including the United States. "The Untouchables" and "Mission Impossible" are two requested American programs.

An age-old form of entertainment still exists, that of gathering to talk and drink beer. The women brew the beer, but the men drink it. The home-brewed beer resembles a thick porridge and can be extremely strong. Alcoholism is a serious social problem.

Commercially brewed Zambian beer is highly regarded. At the Eighth World Beer Selection Contest, held in London in September 1969, two Zambian beers, Castel Lager and Lion Lager, won the top two prizes.

Drugs, other than alcohol, have been present in Zambia since precolonial times and have been used by the people as stimulants and depressants. In recent years, the drug problem has increased in Zambia, but drug abuse has not reached the proportions it has in some other countries, including the United States.

In traditional societies, people frequently gathered to share the meat from a kill. Only recently, however, did eating in restaurants become a possible form of recreation. There are few expensive restaurants in Zambia; those which do exist are mostly in the big tourist hotels. The first Zambian hamburger stand, the Zamby, was opened in November 1971, as the beginning of a chain.

Despite the impact of the missionaries, there are more Africans who continue to practice the spirit worship of the past than those who worship in churches. Among the organized religious communities, the Christian community is the largest. In 1965, several Protestant groups came together to create the United Church of Zambia (UCZ). It is a totally racially integrated church formed from several of the African mission groups, among them Church of Scotland and Methodist, plus the white Copperbelt Free Church Council. President Kaunda is a member of UCZ. The largest Christian groups are UCZ, the Anglicans, and the Roman Catholics. The Jehovah's Witnesses are a group in frequent conflict with the government. Singing the national anthem and saluting the flag are required in Zambian schools. Jehovah's Witnesses believe the Bible forbids such actions, so they do not allow their children to attend public school. A few churches in Zambia, such as the Lumpa sect, have been started by Africans and make use of elements from both African religions and Christianity. The Asians are approximately 66 percent Muslim and the rest Hindu.

Near Kitwe is the Mindolo Ecumenical Foundation. Twenty-three Protestant groups came together to provide this inter-denominational center designed for conferences, training, and research. Many courses, both religious and nonreligious, run throughout the year.

None of Zambia's public holidays are based on traditional celebrations. Her religious holidays are those of Christianity. There are the five associated with Christmas and Easter plus Whit Monday. The day after Christmas is a British holiday called Boxing Day. It was started in England to give the servants who worked on Christmas a day off; frequently, their masters would bring presents or food to them in boxes.

In addition to the six religious holidays, Zambia has seven secular celebrations. Four of them are international holidays—New Year's Day; Labour Day, May 1; Africa Freedom Day, May 25; and Unity Day, first Tuesday in July. Labour Day is observed to honor the working man in countries throughout the world. The latter two are African holidays designated to honor the freedom from colonial rule and the brotherhood of persons on the continent. Heroes Day, first Monday in July, remembers those Zambians who died in battle. Youth Day, August 9, was set aside to recognize the important role Zambian youth play in the nation's development. These holidays may be celebrated with political rallies or parades. But truly elaborate ceremonies accompany Independence Day, October 24. The festivities usually last a week rather than just one day. Perhaps the most colorful activity is a traditional dance contest in Lusaka; dancers come from all parts of the nation to participate.

All countries have symbols which serve to remind their people that they share something in common and that they do—all together—make a whole. A national anthem, a flag, and a coat of arms are three of these unifying symbols.

Zambia's national anthem is *Nkosi Sikelele Africa* (God Bless

Traditional dancing celebrating
Zambia's Independence.

Africa). The flag of Zambia is green with an orange-colored
eagle in the upper right corner above three vertical stripes of
red, black, and orange in the lower right corner. The red is for
the freedom struggle; the black represents the people of Zambia;
the orange, the country's copper and other mineral wealth; and
the green, the natural resources.

The coat of arms carries even more elements of Zambian life.
Black and white wavy lines on a shield represent Victoria Falls.
Above the shield is a hoe, standing for agriculture, and a pick,
standing for mining. The man and woman on either side of the
shield depict the Zambian family. On the ground at their feet is a
mining shaft, a zebra, and, near the bottom, a maize cob, por-
traying mining, wildlife, and agriculture. The eagle soars above,
and below is the national motto which serves to remind Zambians, in the toil and turmoil of forming a country, that, in the
end, the sacrifices and hardships are worthwhile if all Zambians
can proudly face the world united as "One Zambia—One Nation."

Index

About the Author

Eliza T. Dresang has an undergraduate degree from Emory University and a master's degree from U.C.L.A. She has been a teacher and a librarian, compiled a bibliography of African educational research for a Ford Foundation project, and has reviewed African materials for *School Library Journal*. Ms. Dresang lives with her husband and two sons in Madison, Wisconsin, where she works as an elementary school media specialist. The Dresangs have traveled widely in Africa and lived for a year in Zambia. THE LAND AND PEOPLE OF ZAMBIA is Ms. Dresang's first book.